APERITIVO

Kay Plunkett-Hogge

APERITIVO

Drinks and Snacks for the Dolce Vita

Mitchell Beazley

To Antonio Benedetto Carpano,
maker of tinctures and elixirs and
inventor of vermouth — it's all
your fault — I salute you.

And to Fred, the Peter Sellers
to my inner Sophia…

CONTENTS

INTRODUCTION

Let us be honest: who hasn't wanted to be just a little bit Italian? To channel Monica Bellucci in one of those perilously sexy ads for Dolce & Gabbana? Or to glide through Rome like Marcello Mastroianni on a Vespa, wearing an impeccably tailored suit and dark glasses? As I sit in Venice's Piazza San Marco, nibbling *cicchetti* and sipping a Spritz, the dusk settling over the basilica, I realize that this is the perfect evening. Locals and tourists alike imbibe, flirt and promenade.

This is *la dolce vita*.

This is *aperitivo*.

It needn't be Venice. I could be leaning on the counter at All'Antico Vinaio in Florence, drinking a fruity Tuscan red and eyeing a fat *porchetta* sandwich.

I could be savouring an Ambrogino at Bar Zucca in Turin, or nursing a Negroni at Bar Basso in Milan. I could even fight my way to the bar at Federico Fellini's favourite Bar Canova, on the Piazza del Popolo in Rome. It would be the same. Despite each city's divergent character, the *aperitivo* hour still involves a well-made drink, a satisfying, stimulating snack and lashings of Italian *un certo non so che*.

I remember my first encounters with *aperitivo* all too well. Back in my days as a model agent, Milan Fashion Week was obligatory. There, everyone and everything was so achingly *alla moda*, from the lean, mean and hungry agents to the Chicest Shop in the World™, 10 Corso Como. Even the Italian magazine editors seemed to have sharper cheekbones.

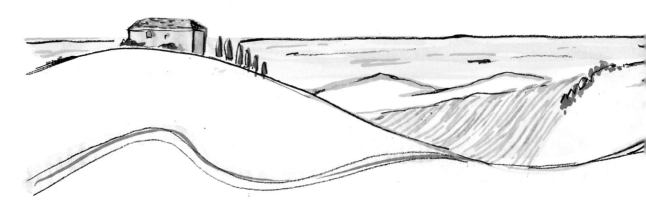

Normally, these kinds of weeks where an entire industry descends on a city tend to be work-hard-play-hard affairs. But Milan is a little bit different. As the work day ground down, the streets began to fill with people and the air began to thrum with conversation. The *aperitivo* hour was upon us, and I sallied forth with Patti, one of the Italian agents, and a couple of the boys we both represented for what would be my first Negroni. It was an almost mystical experience, as though, in one taste, my Britishness fell away – picture Helena Bonham Carter as Lucy Honeychurch in *A Room with a View* as she swoons into the arms of George Emerson. (A good Negroni can do that to a girl.) How could I resist?

While we cannot all be Bellucci or Mastroianni (or even Lucy Honeychurch), there is absolutely no reason at all why we can't bring a little of this spirited Italian ritual home with us. After all, Italian style is very much back in fashion. Italian bars, serving Campari and *cicchetti*, are popping up like mushrooms everywhere, as, much like the tapas trend, people embrace the concept of *aperitivo*.

So let's explore this uniquely Italian take on drinks and snacks and discover exactly how a pre-dinner cocktail becomes *aperitivo*.

THE DRINKS

A LITTLE BIT OF HISTORY...

So where does the Italian habit of *aperitivo* come from? Let's step back in time a moment to meet Antonio Benedetto Carpano, a maker of herbal tinctures and elixirs, and the man widely credited with inventing vermouth as we understand it in Turin in 1786. He was just twenty-two years old. Carpano's original vermouth – white wine infused with over thirty botanicals – caught on as "something for the ladies" to sip before dinner instead of a robust glass of wine. By the mid nineteenth century, most decent bars and restaurants in Turin were serving their own special *aperitivo* concoction to their discerning clientele.

But, while Carpano had created something new, the concept of a drink before dinner goes back much further. The word *aperitivo* comes from the Latin *aperire*, to open. Certainly, the idea of flavouring wine with herbs goes back as far as the Romans too, if not further. And so, it would seem, does the idea of the aperitif. In his book *On Spiritual Knowledge*, which, alas, is not a very early cocktail book, the fifth-century St Diadochus of Photiki writes: "People who wish to discipline the sexual organs should avoid drinking those artificial concoctions which are called 'aperitifs' – presumably because they open a way to the stomach for the vast meal which is to follow." (Clearly old Diadochus knew a thing or two about dating.) So *aperitivi* go back a very long way indeed.

But *aperitivi* as we understand them are comparatively modern. The English idea of the gin and tonic and the French aperitif Dubonnet both emerged in the mid nineteenth century as quinine delivery systems – anything to make the anti-malarial's horrifically bitter taste something to look forward to. The cocktail's rise in popularity is directly connected both to improvements in distilled liquor in general and the ice trade in particular, which also blossomed around the mid nineteenth century. And the fashion in northern Italy for *aperitivi* kicked off at the same time.

The key to it all is industrialization.

Industrialization means more jobs, which means more money in the hands of more people, which in turn leads to the birth of leisure. (It's no accident that the rules of sports began to be codified in the same era.) And leisure means that there's more time for more people to stop and have a drink.

I have a hunch that this is why *aperitivi* are associated more with Italy's industrial north than with the more agricultural south. Frankly, after a hard day in the fields, the last thing you want to do is get yourself all gussied up for a trip to a hipster bar. You want to quench your thirst.

Aperitivi is city drinking – a blast of something bitter-sweet to start the juices flowing before dinner and before whatever else old Diadochus had in mind. But to grasp these drinks' particular Italian qualities, we need to pay attention to two key components that feature either singularly or together in almost every Italian cocktail imaginable: vermouth and Campari.

ON VERMOUTH

Vermouth is a fortified and aromatized wine with an alcohol content of between 14.5% and 22%. The fortified part means that the wine has had a neutral spirit added to it to raise the alcohol levels so that it lasts longer. The aromatized part means that it has been infused with a number of botanical flavouring agents. These, of course, vary by style of vermouth and by manufacturer – the recipes remain closely guarded secrets – but all feature wormwood as a bittering agent, from which the drink derives its name ("vermouth" is a French corruption of the German word *wermut*, which means wormwood).

To keep things simple, people tend to speak of two distinct styles of vermouth. There is dry vermouth, which is similar in colour to white wine, and sweet vermouth, which tends to be red. To make matters a little more complicated, the two styles are sometimes considered to be "French" and "Italian". This is confusing, because most Italian companies make both styles, and more, as do French companies and German companies and so on.

This confusion arises because we forget that Europe's borders have not always been in the same places as they are today. Vermouth's ground zero is Turin. At the time of this drink's invention, Turin was the seat of the House of Savoy, the Duke of which was also rocking the title of King of Sardinia. When Signor Carpano invented his vermouth in 1786, life in Turin (and for the Duke) was relatively stable. But (and I'm abbreviating things quite a lot here) then the French Revolution happened, which shouldn't have been too much of a problem if it wasn't for the fact that states of the Savoy Crown decided to join the First Coalition fighting against the French First Republic, and were resoundingly trounced by Napoleon in 1796.

By the time things settled down some nine years later, and the kingdom (now known as Piedmont-Sardinia) was restored, I think we can assume that those at court in Turin really needed a drink, because vermouth became very popular very quickly. And people began making it across the mainland part of the kingdom, which spread from Livorno in the east as far as Nice in the west and Geneva in the north.

Vermouth's roots cannot be fully divorced from this little slice of history. And it follows from this that, as France reclaimed its eastern borders and the various Italian states unified into one country, their vermouths would evolve differently thanks to the now different cultural and bibulous imperatives that nurtured them.

In Italy, that has resulted in a number of styles and key producers. So it's a question of trying a few to see what you like. In addition to the classic sweet (red) and dry (white) styles, the latter of which subdivides specifically into *bianco* and dry, you will also find Vermouth di Torino, a style that now has protected designation of origin; Vermouth Amaro, which is a sweet vermouth with extra gentian added for bittering; and Vermouth Chinato, which is bittered with cinchona.

MY FAVOURITE ITALIAN VERMOUTHS

How to choose? You must endure the hardship of tasting . . . So find a good independent liquor store (like the wonderful Gerry's in London's Soho) that will let you taste before you buy. This being a book about Italian drinks, I have limited myself here to Italian vermouths. But there are plenty of others from France, Germany, Spain, Britain and the USA. For a proper vermouth adventure, start here, then explore further afield.

PUNT E MES

Just the sight of its label makes my heart skip a beat. The name means "a point and a half". Legend has it that, in 1870, a stockbroker visited the Carpano wine shop in Turin and asked for a drink to reflect the day's share price increase of – you guessed it – one and a half points. So red vermouth and bitters became *punt e mes*. It is pungent and herbal, rich with undertones of orange and a bitter finish.

CINZANO ROSSO 1757

A special edition of their Cinzano Rosso, this is named for the year that Giovanni and Carlo Cinzano started making vermouth. Rich and almost figgy, with hints of citrus, this is delicious on its own and probably my favourite for a Negroni.

STORICO COCCHI VERMOUTH DI TORINO

This is my husband Fred's favourite vermouth, and he is a bit of an expert. Meaning he has imbibed a fair bit of it. Along with herbal undertones and bittersweet citrus, there is a hint of cocoa, rosemary and nutmeg. Spicy and juicy, this is a complex vermouth.

RISERVA CARLO ALBERTI

Named for the King of Piedmont-Sardinia in the 1830s, this was reputedly made for him by his chef. It is cherry led, with vanilla and tonka bean notes. This is my favourite vermouth for sipping before dinner, perhaps with a cube of ice.

MARTINI ROSSO AND RISERVA SPECIALE RUBINO

Established in 1863, Martini is probably the most well known of the vermouths, partly due to the brand's rigorous advertising campaigns through the years. (Let's face it, George Clooney could persuade me to drink pretty much anything. Except for that coffee . . .) Due to added caramel, there is a smoky and spicy undertone to this brew, and I feel it's a little sweeter than the others. However, the Riserva Speciale Rubino iteration is less sweet and has a peppery, red-fruit quality to it.

RISERVA CARLO ALBERTO VERMOUTH EXTRA DRY

A dry and light vermouth, perfect for a dry Martini, or served with soda water and a twist of lemon.

ON CAMPARI

There is nothing else like Campari. It has its imitators. The big Turin drinks companies Martini and Gancia both make things that try to compete with it. Even they fall short of the mark. For Campari is unique.

It belongs in a class of drinks known as digestive bitters. These are distinct from cocktail bitters, which are "non-beverage products", that is to say, you don't drink them on their own. Other digestive bitters include Fernet Branca and Cynar (see page 23), Jägermeister from Germany, Suze from France, Becherovka from the Czech Republic, and so on.

While all have their merits, none hold the yin and yang of bitter and sweet together in such sublime tension as Campari. And none have had such a profound effect on how we drink now. It was invented by Gaspare Campari in the town of Novara, a few miles west of Milan, in 1860. But it wouldn't completely catch on for another fifty years or so, when, in 1915, Davide Campari opened the Bar Camparino in the Galleria Vittorio Emanuele II next to the Duomo in the heart of Milan. With its bespoke hydraulic system to ensure a continuous flow of iced soda water from the cellar to the bar, the place became a sensation.

From this base, Campari began to export, expanding from well-kept Milanese secret to international phenomenon. In this, one cannot escape the power of advertising. Even as early as 1904, when the first Campari factory opened just outside Milan, the drink was presented as both aspirational and something

transgressive. One advertisement dating from that year depicts the concept of bitter as a seductive latter-day highwayman, ready to seduce the woman who sips it at the bar.

Thanks to sex and avant-garde imagery, Campari was the drink of the future – modernity in a bottle, a drink that can marry the urbane charm of David Niven with the untrammelled sex appeal of Salma Hayek and Eva Mendes in one daringly red liquid.

It works, of course, because Campari lives up to the billing. It is urbane. It is sexy. It is daring. And it is modern. Even now. And that remains a concept that is profoundly Italian.

A QUICK GUIDE TO ITALIAN WINE . . .

. . . is almost impossible to write. With something in the region of nearly 400 different grape varieties used to make wine in twenty different regions, which include 73 DOCG wines, 329 DOC wines and who knows how many IGT wines, Italy makes roughly a third of all the world's wine. So it would take a lifetime to grasp the complexities of their oenology. And I am already halfway through mine . . .

Unsurprisingly, the Italians are rather fond of their wine, so even more unsurprisingly, it forms a big part of the *aperitivo* experience. Which means we're going to have to talk about *vino*. Here are a few key pointers:

1. WHAT DO DOCG, DOC AND IGT ACTUALLY MEAN?

These letters describe the Italian appellation system. The Hungarians were the first to come up with a wine classification system in 1730. Even though one of the first protected wine regions was that of Chianti in 1716, one must remember that Italy as we understand it did not exist until 1871. So . . .

The system we have today dates from 1963. It's been tweaked a few times over the years, and it broadly works like this.

DOCG stands for *Denominazione di Origine Controllata e Garantita* (controlled and guaranteed designation of origin), and DOC for *Denominazione di Origine Controllata* (controlled designation of origin). DOCG wines are checked by government officials for quality and have a numbered "seal". DOC wines are not.

IGT stands for *Indicazione Geografica Tipica*, or "indicative of geographical type". Some people say that this is the equivalent of a French *vin de pays*. But it's not. The term was initially invented to classify the Super Tuscan wines like Sassicaia that began to be sold to the public in the early 1970s. At the time of writing, the 2012 vintage retails at around £115 a bottle, which is not what you expect to pay for a *vin de pays*. You can find some exciting wines in this category.

What the alphabet soup is supposed to tell you is that the wines have been made in the manner ascribed to their region and style. For example, a DOCG Chianti must be made with between 70 per cent and 100 per cent Sangiovese grapes. The rest of the wine may be made with Trebbiano and/or Malvasia, but this is not obligatory. It gives the winemaker some wriggle room to make a product uniquely theirs, and to tweak a wine's flavour profile to create consistency year on year.

But . . . it gets more complicated. Because there are other words on the label with their own key meanings.

Classico means that the wine comes from the oldest, most traditional part of the protected region. *Superiore* means that the wine is produced from grapes grown in vineyards with fewer vines per hectare, so of supposedly superior quality, and has

0.5 per cent more alcohol than a corresponding non-*superiore* wine. *Riserva* means that the wine has been aged for a minimum amount of time before bottling. And so on. Everything on the label is there for a reason.

2. NOT ALL ITALIAN SPARKLING WINE IS PROSECCO, AND NOT ALL PROSECCO IS SPARKLING WINE

Prosecco is just a wine named after its region, like Chianti. And, as you'd expect from the above, it has a large DOC and two small DOCGs – Prosecco di Conegliano-Valdobbiadene, where steep hills ensure that the vines are cared for entirely by hand, and Asolo Prosecco Superiore. And not all of it has bubbles.

In fact, there are three levels of fizz to Prosecco: *spumante* (the fizziest), *frizzante* (about half as

fizzy) and *fermo* or *tranquillo* (flat). This last one is comparatively rare, and the only reason they tell you it's *fermo* on the label is so that you know the Prosecco is not "off" but as the winemaker intended.

All of it is made from at least 85 per cent Glera grapes and all of it gains its fizz from a secondary fermentation known as the Metodo Martinotti, which takes place prior to bottling.

Prosecco is not alone in the world of Italian fizz. Though it has fallen from fashion in the wider world, Asti Spumante from Piedmont remains very popular in Italy. Made with the Moscato Bianco grape, it's light and low in alcohol. The Moscato gives it a relative sweetness, but in the good stuff, that's balanced out by acidity. You're more likely to find it served with cake than as an *aperitivo*.

The Trento DOC makes sparkling wines using the Metodo Classico (previously known as the Méthode

Champenoise), where the secondary fermentation happens in the bottle. Like Champagne, they use Chardonnay, Pinot Noir and Pinot Meunier grapes. Unlike Champagne, they also use Pinot Blanc. Perhaps the most famous example is Ferrari Spumante, created by Giulio Ferrari in 1902.

And so on. As with all things Italian wine, there's plenty to choose from. Whichever you choose to serve, please don't pass off your sparkling wine as Champagne if it's not. It's annoying for your guests – trust me, someone will know – and it's insulting to people who care just as much about their wines' distinct charms as the Champenois. We should celebrate sparkly diversity wherever we find it.

3. THERE IS MORE TO ITALIAN WHITE WINE THAN PINOT GRIGIO

In the 1980s and1990s, everyone ordered Chardonnay. Now they order Pinot Grigio. Which, in the more egregious cases, simply tastes like coloured water. I implore you . . . try something different? Please? Like a Grechetto from Sicily, a Pinot Bianco or a Ribolla Gialla from Friuli, a Pampanuto from Puglia. Trust me when I tell you, there's nothing your local wine seller likes more than a customer who says that they want to try something new.

4. THERE IS MORE TO ITALIAN RED WINE THAN CHIANTI

Consumers seem to be more savvy about Italian reds, but it's still quite easy to get caught in a world of Chianti, Valpolicella and Montepulciano d'Abruzzo. Again, there is a lot more diversity and delicacy to be found. I love a big Barolo when I can afford one, but it's good to know, too, that I can find those Nebbiolo flavours in wines across Piedmont and Lombardy. In the latter case, they make extraordinarily light and subtle wines with Nebbiolo in Valtellina, up on the Swiss border. It pays to experiment. Which bring us neatly to . . .

5. HOW DO YOU KNOW WHAT'S GOOD AND WHAT'S NOT?

With wine in general and Italian wine in particular, this is the 50-million-dollar question. After all, when you make a third of the world's wine, you cannot guarantee that every bottle's a winner. Sometimes, the sheer range of choice can seem a little daunting.

I have always been of the opinion that it's good to try new things. I'm also lucky in that I've got to know a couple of excellent wine writers over the years who have never steered me wrong. But even before I started writing about food and drink, I knew there were people I could count on writing in the papers and online, people like Susy Atkins and Jancis Robinson, not to mention Joe Fattorini.

But beyond expert advice, I still hold on to a few hard and fast rules. First, if you like it, it's good. Taste and smell are profoundly subjective. So trust yours. Second, that said, there is such a thing as bad wine – it smells musty or vinegary, depending on what's gone wrong with it. Send it back, or take it back. Even supermarkets should replace a corked bottle. Third, smelling the cork is pointless. It tells you nothing. Fourth, beware of context. One of my most enjoyable wine-drinking experiences took place in an olive grove in Puglia and involved a bottle of Alberobello so rough it could stain your teeth. Had I brought any home, it would have tasted like paint stripper. But that afternoon, it was nectar.

NON-ALCOHOLIC DRINKS

In most countries, the search for a grown-up soft drink can be long and fruitless, and all too often results in club soda. For years, my preferred option has always been soda water with an added dash of Angostura bitters. But Italy has several options for the discerning.

Chinotto is one of the most famous. Made with myrtle-leaved (or chinotto) oranges, it is a bitter-sweet drink invented either by Neri or San Pellegrino (of mineral water fame), depending on whom you choose to believe. In fact, San Pellegrino has this sector of the drinks market pretty well covered. The company also makes Aranciata and a host of other fruit-juice-inflected soft drinks that are not anywhere near as heavily sugared as their transatlantic competitors, as well as Sanbittèr, which tastes like a non-alcoholic Campari.

Not to be outdone, Campari itself make Crodino, though, ironically, I find it rather sweet.

San Pellegrino is not the only water company to make these drinks. San Benedetto makes the delightful Ben's (pictured opposite), which comes in a distinctive tiny bottle and tastes appropriately bitter, with hints of ginger, and which I prefer to lengthen out with ice and soda water.

BAR ESSENTIALS

SWEET VERMOUTH

You cannot make a Negroni (to name just one) without a decent sweet vermouth. Taste a few of them to see which you prefer. (You can find my favourites on pages 13–14.)

DRY OR EXTRA DRY VERMOUTH

Again, taste a few to see which you prefer. There is an ever-increasing range available. A drop or two is essential if you're making a Martini – every good Italian bar will have one.

CAMPARI

There is no excuse for not having a bottle of this iconic ruby-red elixir. And there are very few classic *aperitivo* cocktails made without it.

BITTERS

Bitters can make or break a cocktail. Where once there was only Angostura bitters on the market, now there are hundreds, covering the widest gamut of flavours imaginable. At the very least, you should have a bottle of Angostura. I'd also recommend an orange bitters too – I favour the one from The Bitter Truth. And if the idea of bitters piques your curiosity, there's a whole world of them out there for you to explore.

GIN

Of course you need gin. A bar without gin is like a lawn without grass – not fit for purpose. To my mind, Beefeater is the classic gin. In the words of Carly Simon, nobody does it better. It is the benchmark. But, in a Beefeater-less world, I'd steer you toward the delights of Sipsmith, Plymouth and Portobello Road. Again, taste a few and see what works for you. Eventually, you'll discover that I'm right.

VODKA

I'm not a huge vodka fan. What is vodka if not unfinished gin? That said, you do need it to make a decent Mule, as well as a few other *aperitivi*. And some errant souls prefer it in a Martini.

OTHER DRINKS

There is a plethora of Italian *aperitivi* like Campari and
Aperol on the market. My current favourites are:

BERTO APERITIVO

A pale gold and fragrant combination of orange
blossom, gentian and rhubarb. Serve chilled on its
own or topped up with Prosecco or soda water.

APERITIVO COCCHI AMERICANO

Similar to French Lillet, but more bitter thanks to
the addition of quinine, this is a fortified Moscato
d'Asti wine flavoured with, among other things,
elderberry and a big punch of orange. Delicious
over ice with soda water and a wedge of orange.

CYNAR

Created by the Venetian Angelo Dalle Molle,
this dark bittersweet drink is flavoured with many
herbs and botanicals including artichokes – as
the label makes very clear! Cynar is great served
pre- or post-dinner on its own, and can also be
used as an alternative to Campari in a Negroni
or an Americano.

PROSECCO

Because nothing lifts the spirits like a few bubbles.

LEMONS AND ORANGES

A huge number of drinks require citrus fruit, either as
juice or garnishes. There are precious few limes in
Italian drinks, but lemons and oranges are *de rigueur*.

THE NEGRONI

(Probably the chicest cocktail in the world)

There can be no book on *aperitivi* that does not include, up front, the mighty Negroni. Were this a film, the Negroni would appear above the titles. Were this a play, the Negroni's name would be in lights. Were this a painting, the Negroni would be the drink passed by God to Adam on the Sistine Chapel ceiling. It is a drink whose Italian soul is dressed in the exquisite English tailoring beloved of mid-century Rome.

Quite why this simple drink has proved so utterly beguiling is not so hard to fathom. It is, first of all, very easy to make. Pour three equal measures of gin, Campari and sweet vermouth over some ice; stir briefly to blend; and garnish with a slice of orange. Anyone can do it.

Then there's the colour. That deep red. A colour that could signal danger, or ripeness, or seduction. It is the red of the day's last light, of Sophia Loren's lips, of dreams.

And then there's the taste, a delicate balance between sweet and bitter, enhanced by the botanical aromas of the gin and the orange. This balance is the key to the Negroni, its defining quality.

Not long ago, I acquired a Campari ad from New York (I believe it dates from the early 1950s) that says: "Waterskiing on swans . . . like Campari, an acquired taste . . . you could learn to love it!" It follows this unusual copy with a Negroni recipe, calling it "the world connoisseur's cocktail". The implication is clear: this is sophistication. You may not get it right away, but you can learn to . . . Campari's very bitterness tells you at once that it's a drink for grown-ups. It forms the spine of the cocktail. And it is against this that the other flavours balance. For you can change the gin, you can change the vermouth, but you cannot change Campari. It is constant. As certain in life as death.

And taxes.

As the saying goes.

From here, one must make two decisions. Which gin? And which vermouth?

The gin is the easy bit, at least for me. While those lovely boys at Sipsmith have gone and created their VJOP gin specifically for Negronis, I remain a Beefeater girl through and through. It is the classic London Dry, providing the English tailoring to dress our Italian count. (The Negroni was, after all, allegedly invented for Count Camillo Negroni by the bartender Fosco Scarselli; and the Count, by all accounts, was a very dapper fellow indeed.) Beefeater is a robust and sociable gin and, especially at its export strength of 47% ABV, exhibits delightful citrus notes to complement the stern Campari.

The vermouth brings the frivolity. As in good conversation, frivolity leavens with wit and stops us becoming too serious. It brings light to the dark, sweet to the bitter. As with gin, there are many sweet vermouths to choose from. And, though I have tasted excellent examples from Germany, France and England, I remain convinced that the sweet vermouth in a Negroni must be Italian. The others seem to tip the balance of the drink toward their own (delicious) flavours, as if they're shouting: "Look at me! I'm in a Negroni!"

This, of course, is a matter of taste. And the best way to decide for yourself is by controlled experimentation. Take a couple of chums to a really great bar. Order three Negronis, changing just one element in each one. Taste. Share. Argue. Decide. It's the only way.

Right now, I find myself leaning toward Cinzano 1757 (see page 13).

Which leaves us with two remaining ingredients. The ice must be fresh. So too must the orange.

And the glass.

The glass should be a tumbler. It should feel substantial in your hand. It should suggest weight and seriousness, while the smile on your face shows good humour and bonhomie.

And why not? This is a drink like well-made couture: its very presence makes you stand a little taller, your heart beat with a timbre of elegance. It is a drink with the poise of Baryshnikov, the grace of Carmen Dell'Orefice. It is perfection in liquid form. Sip it, and imagine you're in a L'Oréal campaign.

You are, after all, worth it.

Negroni Chic

KAY'S PERFECT NEGRONI

As Orson Welles said, "The bitters [Campari] are excellent for your liver. The gin is bad for you. They balance each other." He was not wrong.

MAKES 1

25ml (1fl oz) Beefeater gin

25ml (1fl oz) Campari

25ml (1fl oz) Cinzano 1757

a slice of orange or strip of orange zest, to garnish

Over 2 or 3 nicely sized fresh ice cubes, stir together the liquors. Garnish with a generous slice of orange or a strip of orange zest. Drink confidently.

THE PUZO NEGRONI

This comes from James Ramsden, writer, raconteur, radio star, owner of Pidgin in east London and recipient of a freshly minted Michelin star as I type.

James says: "I think one could fairly say that the classic Negroni doesn't need much messing with, but if everything were sacred then life would be pretty dull. This switches out vermouth in favour of the almond-inflected, sweet acidity of Marsala, and works pretty damn well."

Why Puzo? Because the Marsala adds a dangerously Sicilian element. All together now: "Leave the gun. Take the Negroni . . ."

MAKES 1

25ml (1fl oz) gin

25ml (1fl oz) Campari

25ml (1fl oz) Marsala

a sprig of rosemary, to garnish

Stir together the gin, Campari and Marsala in a rocks glass. Add ice. Take a match to the rosemary sprig to create some scented smoke. Blow it out without burning your fingers. Lay atop the glass.

FERGUS HENDERSON'S NEGRONI AS IT SHOULD BE

The year 2016 saw the inaugural Soho Negroni Championship held at the illustrious Quo Vadis Club on London's Dean Street, to which I was invited . . . as one of the judges. (Woo-hoo!) Competition was fierce, as you'd expect, and the duly anointed Supreme Champion on the night was the wonderful Fergus Henderson of St John Restaurant.

I am delighted to share both his recipe and some words of Negroni wisdom: "Negronis: what's not to like? Your first sip, bittersweet and ginny, gives an incredible sense of wellbeing closely followed up by a tingle in the extremities. And this after just one taste! When I was younger I lived in Florence in a vain attempt to learn Italian. After appalling results I was called home. On my last night my favourite bar for Negroni (sadly no longer there) seemed the right spot to head. That night the barman was perfect at capturing and understanding my mood in his execution of the Negroni. Something mystical happened, like a magic, and that evening I learnt a little more about what a Negroni should be."

Fergus gives his recipe in percentages, so the actual size of your drink is up to you . . .

MAKES 1

50% Tanqueray gin

30% Punt e Mes

20% Campari

1 strip of lemon zest

Combine the gin, Punt e Mes and Campari in a rocks glass, stir thoroughly, then add ice cubes. Finish with the lemon strip – *strictly no orange.*

THE AMERICANO

Ah, the Americano – the chic, sophisticated precursor of the magnificent Negroni. It is balanced and light, the perfect drink to have before a Saturday lunch. It is *not* a cup of coffee.

MAKES 1

25ml (1fl oz) gin

25ml (1fl oz) Campari

soda water, to top up

a slice of orange, to garnish

Pour the gin and Campari into a rocks glass filled with ice. Top up with soda water and stir gently. Garnish with an orange slice.

THE NEGRONI SBAGLIATO

Sbagliato means "spoiled" or "wrong". Story has it that, once upon a time, while making a Negroni, a bartender reached for the gin and accidentally grabbed the Prosecco. I find that a rather tall tale. Who in their right mind would keep the Prosecco and the gin side by side? It would make much more sense if our apocryphal barkeep was making an Americano. So maybe, just maybe, we should think of this as an Americano Sbagliato? Just a thought. It is still a damn fine drink.

MAKES 1

20ml (¾fl oz) Campari

20ml (¾fl oz) red vermouth

Prosecco, to top up

a slice or a twist of orange, to garnish

Pour the Campari and the red vermouth over some ice in a rocks glass. Top up with Prosecco. Garnish with an orange slice or twist.

THE SPRITZ

(The aperitivo *that conquered the world)*

If the Negroni is *aperitivo*'s above-the-title movie star, the Spritz is its co-star with equal billing. (And their agents have gone the full twelve rounds over whose name appears on the left of the poster, whose on the right, whose higher, whose lower, in which international territories. If you think this rubbish doesn't matter to people, you've never seen movie actors measuring their trailers . . .)

As with so many drinks, the Spritz's story dates back to the late nineteenth and early twentieth centuries, depending on which story you choose to believe, when one could find a lot of Austrian soldiers wandering around the Veneto. They didn't like the local wine, and took to adding soda water to punch up its acidity. Hence "spritz", which derives from the German word *spritzen*, "to spray".

Soda water is integral to the Spritz's creation, just as it is to the invention of the Americano, whose recipe is first recorded in Ferruccio Mazzon's *Guida al Barman* of 1920. But equally important is the creation of the bitter liqueur, something at which Italy has excelled.

These bitters are not to be confused with cocktail bitters, like Peychaud's or the famous Angostura, though the timings of their invention are broadly the same. While American bartenders and apothecaries were creating their extremely alcoholic bitters, designed to be used in dabs and dashes, Italians were fashioning their bitter liqueurs in the back rooms of coffee houses across Turin – men like Alessandro Martini and Gaspare Campari.

Initially, Italian bitters were used not dissimilarly to their stronger American counterparts. If you ordered a Spritz in the sun-dappled 1950s Italy of *The Talented Mr Ripley*, you'd receive a drink of white wine and soda water, coloured with a dash of the bitter of your choice. It would be another thirty years or so before your bartender would even think of uncorking the Prosecco for you.

The modern Aperol Spritz we know and love today was created at the Bar Capannina in Lido di Jesolo, Venice, in the mid-1990s. In a larger glass, they combined Aperol, Prosecco and ice to immediate success. Such success, in fact, that Aperol has geared its entire brand marketing around it. And to such success that we are forced to ask: can a Spritz be a Spritz without it?

Much as I love Aperol, the answer has to be "yes". What is the Negroni Sbagliato (see page 33) if not some sort of a Spritz? In addition to Aperol, there's the old and glorious standby Campari, Martini Bitter, Contratto Bitter, Berto Aperitivo, Punt e Mes (which manages to blend the genres of bitter, vermouth and amaro into one very sexy bottle) and so on.

In fact, so successful has Aperol been at reviving this sector of the booze biz that long-lost brands are beginning to re-emerge, like the saffron-hued Villacidro from Sardinia, first produced in 1882 and now reborn after falling cataclysmically from local fashion.

So, whether you mix bitter with Prosecco or you take the more traditional approach and use bitter, soda water and white wine, there is now a host of products with which to fix your Spritz. As ever, the key is experimentation. Any good bartender worth their salt will let you have a whiff or a taste of a drink that you don't recognize (all the better to show off their latest discovery; all the better to sell you some). It all just depends on whatever bittersweet mood you're in tonight.

THE SPRITZ

It's 6 pm, and I am sitting at a small table in dappled sunlight outside the Caffè Florian in Venice. It is Italy's oldest café. Deliciously elegant locals have just begun the evening's promenade, gathering to chat and gossip, winding down after a long day. At the bar, there is the clink of ice, the fizz of soda water and the plop of an olive. And then my Spritz arrives, sunset-hued, bittersweet and perfectly cold. *Cin cin*. The Spritz can be made with both Aperol and Campari. If your taste verges on the sweeter side, I would recommend the Aperol. If you prefer that bitter tang, go for the Campari. If you can't decide, you could always go half and half. And, if you're the curious sort, might I recommend seeking out a bottle of the Berto Aperitivo from Turin? It's really rather marvellous.

MAKES 1

60ml (2¼fl oz) Aperol or Campari

120ml (4fl oz) Prosecco

60ml (2¼fl oz) soda water

1–2 large, shiny green olives, to garnish

a wedge of orange, to garnish

Fill a large wine goblet with ice. Pour in the Aperol or Campari. Pour in the Prosecco and top up with soda water. Garnish with an olive, or two if you like, and the orange.

BELLINI CARDINALE

THE BELLINI

THE BELLINI

What drink better conjures up visions of Venice than a classic Bellini? Created by Giuseppe Cipriani, founder of Harry's Bar, in 1948, this peachy dream of a cocktail was named after the pale glow of a saint's toga in a painting by the fifteenth-century Venetian artist Giovanni Bellini. *Bellissimo*, indeed! The peaches must be white peaches . . . their fragrance is second to none.

MAKES 1

2 tablespoons freshly pulped white peach flesh

chilled Prosecco, to top up

Place the peach purée in a chilled Champagne flute or a tall glass. Top up with cold Prosecco. Stir before drinking, to lift the peach. Drink while dreaming of the lagoon . . .

BELLINI CARDINALE

This is a bright and delicious take on a classic Bellini, a marriage of British summertime and Italian sparkle, named *Cardinale* because its colour is reminiscent of a cardinal's cloak . . . You will have to make the purée up front. And you may have some left over, but it keeps beautifully in the fridge for a few days and is heavenly with yogurt for dessert.

MAKES 1

For the purée

75g (2¾oz) strawberries, hulled

175g (6oz) raspberries

a squeeze of lemon juice

1 teaspoon icing sugar, or to taste

For the cocktail

2 tablespoons purée (see above)

chilled Prosecco, to top up

Pass the strawberries and raspberries through a fine-mesh sieve (I use an old-fashioned tamis sieve) into a small bowl to make sure there are no pesky seeds in your drink. Add the lemon juice and sugar and stir well. Taste and add more sugar if needed.

Pop the purée into a chilled Champagne flute or coupe. Top up with cold Prosecco. Stir before drinking.

THE AMBROGINO

This is the signature cocktail at Bar Zucca in Turin, and features Rabarbaro Zucca as its star ingredient. Oddly, while I was familiar with Rabarbaro Zucca from bar shelves across Italy, I had never come across the Ambrogino until I read Marisa Huff's brilliant book *Aperitivo*. Zucca is made with rhubarb. It's delightfully bitter – far less austere than Fernet Branca – and allegedly excellent for the digestion. In the Ambrogino, it's also excellent at piquing the appetite!

MAKES 1

For the syrup

120g (4¼oz) white sugar

120ml (4fl oz) water

½ vanilla pod

For the cocktail

60ml (2¼fl oz) Rabarbaro Zucca

15ml (½fl oz) Campari

15ml (½fl oz) vanilla syrup (see above)

a dash of soda water

½ slice of orange, to garnish

Before you make this cocktail, you will need to make this simple vanilla syrup:

Stir the sugar and water together in a saucepan. Cut the vanilla pod open and scrape out the seeds. Add both pod and seeds to the water, then bring the mixture gently up to a simmer so the sugar dissolves completely. Leave to cool, then store in an airtight jar in the fridge. Strain it before using.

To make the cocktail:

Fill a cocktail shaker with ice and add the liquors and the syrup. Shake like it's your groove thing. Strain into a chilled rocks glass, add the soda water, garnish with the orange, and serve.

If at all possible, try to use a blood orange for the garnish.

THE MI-TO

Created in the 1860s, this marriage of the Campari of Milan and the sweet vermouth of Turin is said to be the precursor of both the Negroni and the Americano (its name is a truncation of Milano and Torino). It is as seductive as both these great cities by night . . .

MAKES 1

15ml (½fl oz) Campari

45ml (1½fl oz) sweet vermouth (I favour Cinzano 1757 for this)

½ slice of orange, to garnish

Put 3 or 4 ice cubes into a rocks glass. Add the Campari and the vermouth. Stir to combine. Garnish with an orange slice.

SEE PAGE 44 FOR A PHOTOGRAPH OF THIS DRINK

THE BICICLETTA

According to urban legend, the Bicicletta is named after a poor chap who after a few too many *aperitivi* rode his bike home rather erratically . . . True or not, the image does make me smile. It is a refreshing and simple drink to make, perfect for a hot summer evening. After a couple, however, I'd recommend that you park the bike and walk home.

MAKES 1

50ml (2fl oz) Campari

50ml (2fl oz) dry white wine

soda water, to top up

a slice of lemon, to garnish

SEE PAGE 44 FOR A PHOTOGRAPH OF THIS DRINK

Stir the Campari and white wine together in a large wine glass. Add ice and top up with soda water. Garnish with a slice of lemon.

THE BICICLETTA

THE ISOLA DEL SOLE

THE MI-TO

THE ISOLA DEL SOLE

My great pals Susanna Mattana and Massimo Usai run Isola del Sole in south-west London, the finest Sardinian establishment this side of the Costa Smeralda. When they asked me to design a cocktail to reflect their beautiful island home, I happily complied – all for a bowl of Susanna's homemade pasta. Here it is. The Mirto or myrtle liqueur captures Sardinia in a bottle.

MAKES 1

25ml (1fl oz) Mirto

very cold Prosecco, to top up

a dash of orange bitters (I favour those from The Bitter Truth)

½ slice of orange, to garnish

Pour the Mirto into a chilled stemmed glass. Top up with cold Prosecco and add a dash of orange bitters. Stir gently and garnish with a jaunty slice of orange. Drink and dream of sunnier shores.

THE QV APERITIVO

A reviving drink from my pal Musa Özgül, the bar manager at Quo Vadis in London's Soho. He says: "Our Chef Patron, Jeremy Lee, came to me one day and asked me if I might create a QV *aperitivo* for our guests to drink with snacks before lunch or dinner. We squeeze amazing fresh orange juice every day in the restaurant, and Campari is our most popular drink in the club. It was quite a simple idea to combine them. Together they are incredibly refreshing and a nice mix of sweet and bitter. I then topped the drink up with Prosecco, because bubbles are always welcome before a meal and it adds a little dry note." Cheers, Musa!

MAKES 1

35ml (1¼fl oz) Campari

35ml (1¼fl oz) freshly squeezed orange juice

chilled Prosecco, to top up

½ slice of orange, to garnish

Pour the Campari and the orange juice into a beautiful coupe glass. Stir. Top up with the cold Prosecco. Garnish with a slice of orange. Add some ice cubes, if you like.

THE GARIBALDI

THE ROMAN MULE

THE ROMAN MULE

The Moscow Mule was invented in Hollywood in the early 1940s to sell ginger beer – Moscow for the vodka, Mule as a bit of a drinking pun because a drink made with ginger ale was, back in the day, called a buck. Make it with bourbon, it becomes a Kentucky Mule; with brandy, a French Mule; and so on. So why, in the name of all things Italian, shouldn't there be a Roman Mule as well? Here it is – as fresh and feisty as Monica Vitti.

MAKES 1

25ml (1fl oz) vodka

50ml (2fl oz) Ramazzotti

ginger beer, to top up

a sprig of mint, to garnish

½ slice of lemon, to garnish

Stir the vodka and Ramazzotti together in a tall glass. Add ice, top up with ginger beer and garnish with a sprig of mint and a slice of lemon.

THE GARIBALDI

This bright orange and aromatic cocktail is named after the great general Giuseppe Garibaldi. Yes, he of the Garibaldi biscuit. Of course, he's really famed for being one of the leading figures in the Italian Risorgimento, which eventually led to the north and south of Italy coming together to form one united country. Hence the Campari from the north and the orange from the south come together in harmony here. Were he alive to know how seriously Anglophones take their biscuits, I don't think the Garibaldi thing would bother him.

MAKES 1

50ml (2fl oz) Campari

orange juice, to top up

a slice of orange, to garnish

Pour the Campari into an ice-filled glass. Top up with orange juice. Stir. Garnish with an orange slice. Sip while watching a Sicilian sunset . . .

GIN AND IT

Short for "gin and Italian", this dates back at least as far as my beloved Martini. Which makes sense – early versions of the Martini were very much "wetter" than those we serve today, and of similar proportions to this. Perhaps that's one of the reasons why it fell out of favour in recent years. But with more and more sweet vermouths available, there is every reason to revisit it. The smooth Italian of the vermouth just sidles up to kiss the very British gin and make her blush. Sophisticated and slick, this drink has a kick.

MAKES 1

60ml (2¼fl oz) gin

30ml (1¼fl oz) red vermouth

a dash of orange bitters

a twist of lemon, to garnish

Stir the gin and vermouth together over ice and strain into a cocktail glass, or pour the liquors over some ice in a rocks glass. Add a dash or two of the orange bitters. Stir. Garnish with a lemon twist. Either way, it's delicious.

THE FOOD

KITCHEN STAPLES FOR THE DOLCE VITA . . .

OLIVE OIL

Good olive oil is essential. Try out as many as you can and find your favourite. I like to have two regular olive oils on the go and one excellent extra virgin olive oil for dressings and drizzling. At the moment I am a little in love with Olio del Castello in its chic bottle.

PARMIGIANO REGGIANO

Never be without a block of this in the fridge. Eat it alone with a glass of Prosecco or grate it over a plate of buttery, peppery pasta. Please, please, never buy that grated stuff in pots . . .

TUNA

Find the best you can, preferably packed in olive oil, though sunflower oil will do at a pinch. (I find the ones in brine are tasteless and the texture is odd.) My favourite Italian brands are Rio Mare and Palmera. They are available in good Italian delis and online, and of course the Spanish brand Ortiz is excellent.

ANCHOVIES

Again, quality equals flavour. I always have a half-dozen cans or jars in the cupboard. It's so easy to add a couple of anchovies to gravies, pasta sauce, roasts and butter for a real kick of flavour. Or simply serve them with bread and unsalted butter.

CANNED BEANS

Beans, glorious beans – cannellini, borlotti, chickpeas. Yes, dried beans have a better texture, etc., etc., but I frequently forget to soak them when I need them. And then there's the time and convenience thing. So . . . canned beans. Easy to gussy up into salads and dips.

CANNED TOMATOES

Quality canned tomatoes – whole or chopped, it's up to you.

PASTA

I like to have three pasta types at hand – capellini, because it is so light and quick to cook; spaghetti or linguine (interchangeably), because everyone loves them; and a shape. Orecchiette is my favourite – those little "ears" catch all the saucy goodness. My favoured brands are Rummo and Giuseppe Cocco. The latter is cut on bronze dies, leaving a rough surface that is great at catching sauce.

SEA SALT

And by this I mean a good, coarse sea salt. I tend to prefer it for the texture, but also you can just grind it gently in a pestle and mortar and voilà! Fine sea salt.

WINE

There's a fair bit of wine in Italian cooking, both red and white. And there's absolutely no reason why you shouldn't have a glass while you're cooking. So enjoy it!

RISOTTO RICE

Choose the one you like. Arborio is the variety most widely available, but it needs careful tending or it might turn a bit mushy. Carnaroli is the best at retaining its grain integrity, while Vialone Nano – my favourite – gives a very creamy finish.

VINEGARS

White balsamic, and a dark if you like. A good red and a good white wine vinegar, too.

LEMONS

Every kitchen (and bar) should have lemons.

GARLIC AND ONIONS

Plentiful supplies hang on my walls!

CAPERS

I keep jars of both small capers and the larger caper berries in my fridge.

FRESH AND DRIED HERBS

Good dried oregano is a must. And I keep fresh parsley in a jam jar of water within easy reach. All others I buy as needed.

INTRODUCTION TO THE MENUS

With Italian food, regionality is everything – in no other food culture does the slightest shift in locality have so much impact on cooking and eating. So it follows that, even though *aperitivo* is a northern Italian urban concept, the food will differ from city to city. On the following pages, I have gathered together dishes that are typical of Milan, Turin, Rome, Venice and Florence. (This is not to be dictatorial – you should serve what you like with what you like.) Each menu includes something raw, something cooked, something you can do ahead of time – the last thing you want is a menu where you have to make everything at the last second.

There are also some dishes lurking here that could be a first course or side dishes for a bigger meal. Pasta, for example, is not traditionally served as an *aperitivo*, neither are risotto or risi e bisi, but sometimes it's fun to break the rules. Isn't it . . . ?

MILAN

**PANE ALLE OLIVE
DI SUSANNA**
page 198

POLPETTE DI TACCHINO
page 127

**"PATATINE FRITTE" DI POLENTA
AL ROSMARINO**
page 152

SUPPLÌ AL TELEFONO
CON PORCINI E TARTUFO
page 159

TURIN

TARTARE DI VITELLO
page 121

BAGNA CAUDA
page 103

ROME

**BUCCE DI MELANZANE
MARINATE AL PEPE**
page 179

**ROTOLI DI
BRESAOLA CON
ASPARAGI ARROSTO**
page 122

**RISOTTO AL FEGATO DI POLLO
E ROSMARINO**
page 129

CAPELLINI CON GAMBERI
GRIGI, AGLIO E CAPPERI
page 115

PANZANELLA
page 151

BACCALÀ MANTECATO
page 98

SARDE EN SAOR
page 97

RISI E BISI
page 161

VENICE

FRITTO MISTO
page 90

TRAMEZZINI
pages 76 –7

FRED'S CARPACCIO
page 130

FLORENCE

SPIEDINI DI PORCHETTA
page 143

SALSA VERDE
page 144

FAGIOLI ALLA MALTESE
page 176

CROSTINI DI FEGATO DI POLLO
page 83

PINZIMONIO
page 70

AN ANTIPASTI PLATTER

Ah, the antipasti platter – *grazie mille, Italia!* This is probably the perfect way to eat while you're drinking. A little bit of ham, a little bit of cheese, olives, artichoke hearts – it's perfect, it's simple, it's low maintenance when it seems high maintenance. In short, it's effortless, like classical Italian style. (Let's face it, a perfectly sliced sliver of prosciutto di Parma is just as elegant as a perfectly cut Pucci dress . . .)

There aren't any real rules to assembling a good platter of antipasti – just add lots of what you like. I suggest you hop on your Vespa (or the number 22 bus) and head to your nearest Italian deli to pick up a few things . . . I like to include 4–6 of the following:

SALAMI: There are so many types, from all across Italy. Among my favourites are:

- Milano: finely chopped, smooth, mildly peppery pork-based sausage.
- Calabrese: spicy and fatty – just gorgeous.
- Finocchiona: in a thick white casing, this salami is full of fennel. It must be sliced very thinly – if you manage to get a whole one, ask your local deli to slice it for you.

PROSCIUTTO CRUDO: Dry cured ham that is made using the hind legs of heritage-breed pigs, which are salted and then hung. The most famous are prosciutto di Parma and prosciutto di San Daniele. They are both excellent, though the San Daniele has a sweeter flavour because less salt in the curing process.

PROSCIUTTO COTTO: Simple boiled ham, sometimes flavoured with herbs and spices.

MORTADELLA: Smoked sausage from Bologna – this is where the American term "baloney" comes from. It is very smoothly minced pork and beef, dotted with pieces of pork fat. To be a real mortadella, the sausage must contain 15 per cent pork fat.

BRESAOLA: Hailing from Lombardy, this is dark ruby-red salted and air-dried beef. Delicious with rocket, Parmesan and lemon juice.

GORGONZOLA CHEESE: Made from full-fat cows' milk in Lombardy and Piedmont, this is a blue-veined cheese with a crumbly texture and a sharp taste. Great with a handful of walnuts.

PECORINO ROMANO: Salty, sharp sheep's milk cheese from Lazio and Sardinia, with a long history. Ancient scribes from Pliny the Elder to Hippocrates raved about the stuff, and it was a staple of the Roman soldier's diet. I love it with a Negroni – something about its saltiness makes it a perfect pairing.

TALEGGIO: I always have a chunk of this funky, stinky cows' milk cheese from Lombardy ready to smear on bread. Someone once said there is something almost "beefy" about its flavour – and I agree.

MOZZARELLA DI BUFALA: Probably the most famous Italian cheese after Parmesan. I must say, I'd usually serve this separately with some figs or perfectly ripe tomatoes, basil and good olive oil, but it's up to you . . .

PEARS DRIZZLED WITH HONEY: On the first night of our honeymoon in Rome, the restaurant was closed (well, it was Sunday, but still, HORRORS!). The bartender kindly served us this along with a selection of cheeses. I was smitten. And given the honey, I suppose it was rather apt.

FIGS OR PLUMS: One rule, and one rule only: they must be RIPE.

BREAD: A good crusty loaf of your choosing – or you could bake Susanna's bread on page 198.

OLIVES: Choose your favourites – mine are French, I'm afraid: Picholines. Just perfect! But taste the different types and pick your own olive hero.

ARTICHOKE HEARTS: These usually come from a jar or a can. Try to find the roasted ones, and serve with a drizzle of oil and some parsley.

ROASTED RED PEPPERS: You could buy these ready roasted in a jar, but they are so easy to make.

4 red peppers
3 tablespoons extra virgin olive oil
sea salt and freshly ground black pepper

Holding them with tongs, one at a time, place the peppers over the gas flame of your cooker. Turn them a few times until they are completely charred and blackened. If you don't cook on gas, you can also char them under a hot grill. Place the peppers in a bowl and cover with clingfilm, or put them in a plastic bag and seal. Leave for about 30 minutes – the steam will make them easier to peel. Once they are cool, peel them gently and cut into strips, removing the seeds and stalks. Dress with the olive oil, and salt and pepper.

PINZIMONIO

This isn't really a recipe. It's just a classy Italian version of crudités, Tuscan in origin, and popular in the autumn when the new olive oil has been pressed. So, when you serve this, make sure you use the best olive oil you can afford because that's the whole point of *pinzimonio*. The great plus, I think, is that this is a thing that makes everybody happy. It's delicious. Your health-nut pals will be delighted – heaven forfend that they should have to eat something fried – and everyone can tick off one of their 5-a-day without really noticing it. And you won't have to bust a gut in the kitchen.

Use whatever vegetables are in season, or just your favourites. I tend to plump for:

Carrots, peeled, halved and quartered (baby ones in season would be lovely)

Baby sweet peppers, halved and deseeded

Red and green chicory, sliced in half

Romanesco broccoli, cut into florets

Radishes

Spring onions

Green beans, trimmed

Celery sticks

To serve

olive oil

sea salt

freshly ground black pepper

Arrange the vegetables artfully on a beautiful platter or tray.

Pour your favourite olive oil into one bowl and, in another, mix sea salt with freshly ground black pepper. You could also add some thyme leaves, or finely chopped rosemary leaves.

Let your guests choose their veggies and dip them first into the oil, then into the seasoned salt.

Buonissimo!

FICHI E PROSCIUTTO

Figs and prosciutto

Some folks may ask why I have included a recipe for something so, so simple. Surely it's just that: some figs and some ham. Perhaps. But there are a couple of cardinal rules. And, as your guide to *aperitivi*, I feel it would be remiss not to point them out. The figs must be the ripest and juiciest you can find. If they're dry or hard, don't bother. And when I say "the ripest and juiciest", we're talking about the kind of fig that would have distracted Adam and Eve from covering themselves with fig leaves. If the figs are lacklustre in any way, make something else. Or use another fruit. Mangoes or melons are wonderful substitutes. The prosciutto, too, has to be of the best quality you can afford. And sliced paper thin. If you can get to a good Italian deli, do so. So, no, this is not a recipe per se. It is a reminder that, with this kind of simplicity, you do not mess about with shoddy ingredients.

SERVES 6

12 good figs

12 slices of prosciutto

Drape the ham on a beautiful board or plate and place the fruit beside it.

Let everyone tear the figs and roll the pieces in prosciutto while licking the juices off their fingers.

TRAMEZZINI AND A SPRITZ . . .

Picture yourself in the Piazza San Marco. You are tired from a day of seeing the sights of Venice. But how could you possibly be tired of this place? Like Katharine Hepburn in *Summertime*, you are beguiled by the city itself. The sun is going down. The canals shimmer in the peach-hued evening light. People have begun to promenade, sashaying by with a flair that only Italians have. And in the distance, like a mirage, a uniformed waiter approaches with a silver tray. Upon it are a small bucket of ice and a frosty glass of Aperol Spritz, its orange and olive garnish gleaming like a Renaissance brooch. And alongside that lies a selection of triangular sandwiches, almost doll-like in their daintiness. This is Venice. And these are *tramezzini* . . .

Tramezzini are, for want of a better way of putting it, the same sort of sandwiches you might have with afternoon tea in England, except they are served with drinks. They are made with soft white sliced bread, which sometimes underwhelms those who have come to revere all things Italian food as artisan (don't worry . . . it WORKS). And they are wildly popular across northern Italy, especially in the Veneto. You will find them everywhere, from vending machines to the chicest speakeasy.

The word *tramezzino* translates as "a little something in between". It was coined by the poet Gabriele D'Annunzio to replace the word *sandwich* because . . . well . . . Mussolini banned it. Along with all the other non-Italian words in the language. Charming.

The following recipes are simply ideas for you to mess around with. So you should let your imagination run wild as you think up your own *tramezzini* fillings.

All recipes make 4 triangles or *tramezzini* . . .

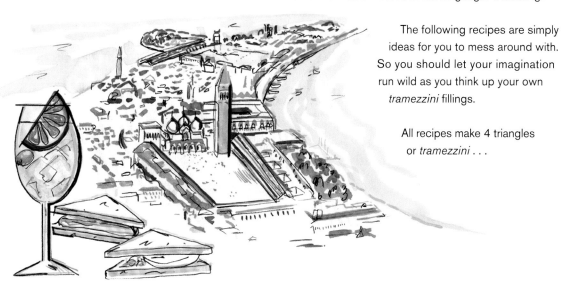

TONNO, UOVA E OLIVE

Tuna, egg and olives

120g (4¼oz) tuna in oil, drained

2 tablespoons mayonnaise

a squeeze of lemon juice

4 slices of packaged white bread, crusts removed

4–6 pitted black olives, halved

1 hard-boiled egg, shelled and sliced

sea salt and freshly ground black pepper

In a small bowl, mix together the tuna and the mayonnaise. Season with the lemon juice, salt and pepper.

Layer on to 2 slices of the bread. Dot the olive halves on top, then add the egg slices. Season again if you like. Top with the remaining 2 slices of bread. Cut in half diagonally to form 4 triangles.

POLLO E CAPPERI CON AÏOLI

Chicken and capers with aïoli

1 chicken breast, grilled or poached

2 tablespoons garlic mayonnaise

1 tablespoon capers, drained and chopped

½ tablespoon chopped fresh flat-leaf parsley

4 slices of packaged white bread, crusts removed

sea salt and freshly ground black pepper

Shred the chicken breast. Pop the chicken into a bowl and add the mayonnaise, capers and parsley. Season with salt and pepper.

Layer on to 2 slices of the bread. Top with the remaining 2 slices. Cut diagonally into 4 triangles.

SEE PAGE 75 FOR A PHOTOGRAPH OF THESE TRAMEZZINI

PROSCIUTTO COTTO E FUNGHI SALTATI

Ham and sautéed mushrooms

1 tablespoon olive oil

100g (3½oz) mushrooms, sliced

1 garlic clove, bashed in its skin

1 tablespoon chopped fresh flat-leaf parsley

4 slices of packaged white bread, crusts removed

1 tablespoon mayonnaise

4 slices of good ham

sea salt and freshly ground black pepper

Heat the oil in a heavy-based frying pan. Add the mushrooms and sauté until they have let go of their liquid. Add the garlic and stir in well. Season with salt and pepper. Remove from the heat and leave to cool. Once cool, remove the garlic clove and stir in the parsley. Taste and adjust the seasoning if needed.

Spread 2 slices of the bread with mayonnaise. Layer on the ham and mushrooms. Place the remaining 2 slices of bread on top. Cut each pair diagonally into triangles.

ARROSTO DI MANZO CON RAFANO E CRESCIONE

Roast beef with horseradish and watercress

1 tablespoon mayonnaise

1 tablespoon crème fraîche

¼ teaspoon English mustard

1 teaspoon grated horseradish

a squeeze of lemon juice

4 slices of packaged white bread, crusts removed

2–4 slices of rare roast beef

a small handful of watercress

sea salt and freshly ground black pepper

Mix together the mayonnaise, crème fraiche, mustard, horseradish and a squeeze of lemon juice. Season with salt and pepper.

Spread this on to 2 slices of the bread. Top with the slices of beef. Add a few leaves of watercress. Place the remaining 2 slices on top. Cut them in half on the diagonal.

BRUSCHETTE E CROSTINI

Let's be honest: these are things on toast. But what toast! Because . . . well . . . what bread!

Bread is the key to a decent *bruschetta*. And nowhere is this better demonstrated than with my all-time favourite. Grill or toast a slice of really great white bread – ideally over the barbecue coals while you rest the meat you just cooked. Rub the bread with the cut side of half a garlic clove. Drizzle it with extra virgin olive oil. Sprinkle it with some fresh thyme leaves and sea salt. Close your eyes. And bite into it. The crunch . . . the prickle of great olive oil . . . the tang of raw garlic . . . the smoke of the grill . . . all set against little fireworks of salt and herbs. If bread is the stuff of life, then this is its ambrosial form, made for the gods alone.

Of course, you can top both *bruschette* and *crostini* with all manner of things. (The only real difference between the two, as far as I can tell, is size. *Bruschette* are larger, and their name derives from the Italian *bruscare*, to roast over coals. *Crostini* just means "little toasts", exactly what they are.) As with *tramezzini*, set your imagination free to top them with whatever you please. Here are some thoughts to start you off.

AVOCADO CON PESTO DI RUCOLA

Avocado on toast – Italian style!

I still remember my first avocado. Our Texan friends the Kellys brought some back to Bangkok, where my family was living at the time, in about 1972. One taste and I was hooked. Guacamole, avocado on toast, you name it, I'm in there. The addition of rocket pesto, however, is all down to my friend Massimo, whose obsession with avocado rivals even my own (both are trumped by his obsession with Arsenal Football Club. . .). It works thanks to avocado's long friendship with spice, and the peppery fieriness of the rocket makes a perfect foil for the creamy fruit.

MAKES 1 LARGE TOAST

a large handful of rocket, plus extra to garnish (optional)

1 tablespoon toasted pine nuts

1 tablespoon grated Parmesan cheese

olive oil, to emulsify

1 avocado

1 large slice of toast or grilled bread

a pinch of dried chilli flakes (optional)

sea salt and freshly ground black pepper

SEE PAGE 79 FOR A PHOTOGRAPH OF THESE CROSTINI

Put the rocket, pine nuts and Parmesan into a mini chopper or food processor. With the motor going, add olive oil until you have a consistency you like. Season with salt and pepper.

Mash the avocado roughly. Pile it on to the bread and pour over the rocket pesto. Garnish with some chilli flakes and a few extra leaves of rocket if you like.

GRANCHIO E FINOCCHIO

Crab and fennel

The sweetness of the crab works beautifully with the fennel's anise.

MAKES 1 LARGE TOAST

60g (2¼oz) crabmeat

1 tablespoon good-quality mayonnaise

½ tablespoon finely chopped fennel

a good squeeze of lemon juice

1 large slice of toast or grilled bread

sea salt and freshly ground black pepper

Mix the crabmeat, mayo, fennel and lemon juice together very gently, and season with salt and pepper. Pile on top of the toast and garnish with a fennel frond or two if you have some.

POMODORO E BASILICO

Fresh tomato and peppery basil with a dash of fruity olive oil

MAKES 1 LARGE TOAST

1 large and juicy tomato, chopped

1 garlic clove, finely chopped

a handful of fresh basil, torn, plus extra to garnish (optional)

1 tablespoon extra virgin olive oil

1 large slice of toast or grilled bread

sea salt and freshly ground black pepper

Mix the tomato, garlic, basil and olive oil together gently, and season with salt and pepper. Taste and add more seasoning if you need it.

Pile it on to the toast and garnish with extra basil if you like.

CROSTINI DI FEGATO DI POLLO

Creamy chicken livers with onion and capers

These are the only *crostini* in this section – really they're just a smaller version of *bruschette* – because, well, unless you're gutting your own chickens, it's hard to buy chicken livers in small quantities. So I'm giving a bulk recipe. The cooked mixture will keep in the fridge for 3–4 days in a sealed container.

MAKES ABOUT 450G (1LB)

400g (14oz) chicken livers, trimmed and chopped

2 tablespoons butter

4 tablespoons olive oil

1 onion, finely chopped

1 garlic clove, finely chopped

2 sprigs of fresh rosemary, leaves only, finely chopped

2 sprigs of fresh thyme, leaves only

1–2 tablespoons capers, drained

50ml (2fl oz) Marsala

a dash of lemon juice

sea salt and freshly ground black pepper

toasted bread, to serve

Season the livers with salt and pepper.

Heat half the butter and half the olive oil in a wide frying pan. Add the onion and cook until softened. Then add the garlic, herbs and capers. Cook for a minute or two, then scoop out and set aside.

Wipe the pan clean with kitchen paper. Add the rest of the butter and olive oil and heat until the butter is melted. Put in the livers and cook through, turning every now and then to caramelize them a little. Put the onion mix back into the pan. Add the Marsala and the lemon juice and bubble for a few minutes.

Remove from the pan to a food processor. Pulse for a few minutes. Leave to cool slightly.

Serve smeared generously on to toasted bread.

PISELLI DOLCI E RICOTTA

Sweet garden peas and creamy ricotta with a hint of mint

This is simple and summery, and, because we are using frozen peas, it provides a touch of sunshine all year round.

MAKES 1 LARGE TOAST

2 tablespoons frozen peas, defrosted

3 tablespoons ricotta

½ tablespoon chopped fresh mint

1 large slice of toast or grilled bread

sea salt and freshly ground black pepper

In a bowl, gently mix the peas, ricotta and mint together. Season with salt and pepper to taste. Spoon on to the toast and serve.

SEE PAGE 79 FOR A PHOTOGRAPH OF THESE CROSTINI

ACCIUGHE E BURRO

Anchovies and butter

Why didn't I think of this? One day, I stopped by Bibo, a lovely Italian restaurant and bar in Putney, south-west London, for a quick lunch, and there this was on the menu. It is the perfect snack. Of course, it doesn't work if you use any old bread, any old butter, any old anchovy. Quality ingredients make it work. So if you can't be bothered to find them, don't bother.

MAKES 1

a good pat of unsalted butter

2–4 good-quality canned anchovies

1 slice of good bread

Place the butter and the anchovies on a plate alongside the bread. Pour a glass of wine or make an Americano (see page 32).

Smear a little butter on the bread and top with a piece of the anchovy. Marvel at the sheer deliciousness.

In an ideal world, the bread should be still warm, or very lightly toasted.

SEAFOOD

CALAMARI ALLA GRIGLIA CON SALSA AÏOLI AI CAPPERI E LIMONE

Grilled squid with lemon and caper aïoli

Grilled squid is one of my absolute favourite things. And there are two nationalities, in my opinion, who cook it perfectly: the Thais and the Italians. In the former case, you can expect it to be served with a fiery *nam jim seafood*. In Italy, I've often had it like this. Honestly, I don't know which one I prefer.

SERVES 4-6

500g (1lb 2oz) cleaned squid, halved if small, or cut into pieces if larger, including tentacles

2 tablespoons olive oil

sea salt and freshly ground black pepper

lemon wedges, to serve

For the mayonnaise

4 garlic cloves, peeled

a good pinch of sea salt

2 large fresh egg yolks

125ml (4fl oz) extra virgin olive oil

125ml (4fl oz) olive oil

1 teaspoon lemon juice

1 heaped tablespoon capers, drained and chopped

First, make the mayonnaise. I like to use a pestle and mortar – see page 106 if you would prefer to use a food processor. Warm your mortar with a splash of hot water, and dry well. Crush the garlic in the mortar with the sea salt, getting it as smooth as you can. Add the egg yolks and combine, stirring and pressing, always in the same direction.

When you have a silky amalgam, start adding the olive oil a drop at a time, stirring and pressing constantly.

Once the mixture has thickened and starts to feel more "jellyish", you can add more of the oil, in a thin stream, continuing to stir with the pestle until you have a nice wobbly mayonnaise. Add the lemon juice and capers and stir to combine. Taste and adjust the seasoning. Serve at room temperature.

To cook the squid, heat a griddle pan on a high flame until blisteringly hot. Lightly oil and season the squid. Then slap them on to the griddle and cook for about 2–3 minutes, turning them once so you get some nice char marks and the squid is cooked through and slightly golden.

Serve straight away, with wedges of lemon and the mayonnaise.

TIP: You can make the mayonnaise ahead of time if you like. Just make sure you keep it in the fridge. It will last for a couple of days.

FRITTO MISTO

Mixed fried seafood

Crisp, lightly battered seafood, served preferably al fresco with wedges of lime and a Bellini... oh, Venice, how I love thee! I have based this recipe on the one from Da Romano in Giancarlo and Katie Caldesi's wonderful book *Venice: Recipes Lost and Found*. Do buy it – it's a delight.

SERVES 4-6

vegetable oil, for deep-frying

750g (1lb 10oz) mixed seafood – big prawns with shells on, squid cut into rings, chunks of firm white fish

400ml (14fl oz) milk

400g (14oz) '00' flour

sea salt

lemon wedges, to serve

Heat the oil to 180°C (350°F) in a deep-fat fryer.

Put the seafood into a bowl of milk for a minute or two.

Shake off the excess milk, then pop the pieces of seafood into the flour and coat well, shaking off any excess. Drop them gently into the oil and fry until cooked through, crisp and golden brown – about 2–3 minutes.

Drain on kitchen paper and serve piping hot, with a sprinkling of salt and lemon wedges.

INSALATA DI PUNTARELLE

Puntarelle salad with anchovy and caper dressing

Traditionally served in Rome as *puntarelle alla Romana*, this salad would not normally include capers, but I like the added pop of sharpness they bring against the bitter leaves and the salty anchovies. Puntarelle is a wonderful bitter plant that is ideal for salads. It is not always easy to find in northern climes, so if you cannot track it down, feel free to use white chicory instead.

SERVES 4-6

1 head of puntarelle

4 anchovy fillets

2 garlic cloves, peeled

3 tablespoons red wine vinegar or lemon juice

6 tablespoons extra virgin olive oil

1–2 tablespoons capers, drained

sea salt and freshly ground black pepper

Trim the outer dark and straggly leaves off the puntarelle. Either discard or keep to sauté with some garlic, as you would greens. Cut the remaining stems and bulb lengthways into strips and then again into strips of about 8cm (3 inches). Soak them in a bowl of iced water for an hour or two, until crisp and curling a little.

To make the dressing, chop the anchovies into small pieces and mash them together with the garlic in a pestle and mortar. Season with black pepper and stir in the red wine vinegar or lemon juice. Then whisk in the extra virgin olive oil a little at a time until you have an emulsion – you may not need all the oil.

Drain the puntarelle and thoroughly spin or pat it dry. Stir in the capers. You shouldn't need any salt, thanks to the anchovies, but taste it and add some if necessary. Serve at once.

COZZE RIPIENE

Mussels stuffed with breadcrumbs and herbs

I first had these stuffed mussels at a beachside café on the Adriatic Coast. And I was promptly struck by the wonderful combination of textures — the soft, creamy mussels juxtaposed with the crunch of the toasty breadcrumbs, all set off by the fire of Puglian chilli. As a plus, each morsel comes in its own handy container. Which makes them perfect to enjoy with a drink.

SERVES 4–6

1kg (2lb 4oz) mussels

100ml (3½fl oz) white wine

200ml (7fl oz) water

3 tablespoons olive oil

lemon wedges, to serve

For the stuffing

100g (3½oz) breadcrumbs

a large handful of fresh parsley, finely chopped

2–4 small dried peperoncini, crumbled

4 garlic cloves, finely chopped

sea salt and freshly ground black pepper

First clean the mussels, pulling off any excess beard you may find sticking out of their shells.

Pour the white wine and the water into a large pan and bring to the boil. Add the mussels, discarding any that are open, and bring back to the boil. Place a lid on and steam until they are open. Drain the mussels and discard any that are still closed. Leave to cool long enough for you to be able to handle them.

Preheat the oven to 200°C (400°F), gas mark 6.

Mix together the breadcrumbs, parsley, chilli and garlic. Season with salt and pepper — be careful with the salt, as the mussels will already have a salinity to them.

Once you can handle the mussels, remove the top shells by gently twisting, leaving the mussel meat attached to the bottom shell. Place them on one or two large baking trays. Top each mussel with a generous helping of the crumb mixture. Drizzle all over with the olive oil.

Bake for about 10–15 minutes, or until fragrant, crisp and golden.

Serve with lemon wedges on the side.

SEE OVERLEAF FOR A PHOTOGRAPH OF THIS DISH

SARDE EN SAOR

Soused sardines

This traditional dish hails from the Veneto. Its sweet and sour, or *agrodolce*, flavour is delightfully refreshing.

SERVES 4-6

4 tablespoons raisins

125ml (4fl oz) white wine

100g (3½oz) '00' flour

200ml (7fl oz) olive oil

8–12 fresh sardines, filleted

1 onion, sliced

250ml (9fl oz) white wine vinegar

1 bay leaf

6 strips of lemon peel

2 teaspoons coriander seeds

4 tablespoons pine nuts, toasted

sea salt and freshly ground black pepper

chopped fresh flat-leaf parsley, to garnish

crusty toasted bread, to serve

Pop the raisins into the white wine. If you can do this the night before, all the better.

Season the flour with salt and pepper.

Heat all but 3 tablespoons of the oil in a wide, heavy frying pan.

Gently dust the sardines with the seasoned flour and fry until crisp and cooked through. Remove and set aside to drain on kitchen paper. Discard the oil, then wipe out the pan.

Pour the remaining olive oil into the clean frying pan and heat. Fry the onions until softened nicely. Add the vinegar, bay leaf, lemon peel and coriander seeds. Bring to the boil and simmer for a minute or so. Add the raisins and pine nuts and bubble for 1 minute. Remove from the heat.

Start layering the sardines in a glass dish. A layer of sardines, then some raisins, onions and pine nuts, then sardines again, finishing off with a final sprinkle of raisins, onions and pine nuts. Pour the vinegar sauce over the top.

Once it has cooled a little, cover the whole dish with clingfilm and refrigerate for at least 24 hours.

Scatter with chopped parsley and serve with crusty toasted bread.

BACCALÀ MANTECATO

Venetian fish mousse

This creamy, delicate mousse from Venice is usually made with dried cod (known as stockfish) rather than salted cod, but I prefer it this way – and not just because it's easier to find the latter if you're not in the Veneto! Traditionally, one beats the mixture by hand in a bowl with a wooden spoon but, to be honest, it takes an awfully long time and I find that my food processor does all the hard work very well . . . Make sure to soak your cod according to the packet instructions.

MAKES ABOUT 20-24 PIECES

250g (9oz) boneless salt cod, soaked

¼ lemon

3 garlic cloves, peeled

2 bay leaves

125ml (4fl oz) olive oil

sea salt and freshly ground white pepper

a selection of chicory leaves and toasted bread, to serve

chopped fresh parsley, to garnish

Drain the salt cod and rinse in cold water. Place in a large saucepan and cover with more cold water. Add the lemon, garlic and bay leaves. Bring to the boil and simmer for about 20 minutes, or until the cod is very tender – you want it to break apart or flake easily. Strain the fish, discarding the lemon and the bay leaves, but reserving the garlic cloves and about 100ml (3½fl oz) of the cooking water.

Pop the fish and the garlic into a food processor and switch on. As the motor is running, add the olive oil in a thin stream until the mixture is amalgamated and silky. It's a bit like making mayonnaise. Add a little of the cooking water if it seems too thick – you want a mousse-like consistency.

You can chill it, but I like to serve it at room temperature.

Pile on to toasted bread or into individual chicory leaves and garnish with a little chopped parsley.

INDIVIA E POMODORO CON SALSA TONNATA

Chicory and tomato with tonnato sauce

Traditionally *salsa tonnata* – which is essentially a tuna mayonnaise – is made with fresh eggs and served cold. You'll often find it atop thinly sliced veal, making the classic Piedmont dish of *vitello tonnato*. Here I have, through greed and laziness, created a cheat's *tonnato* sauce using store-bought mayonnaise. And I've cribbed the idea of putting it on tomatoes from the excellent *Canal House Cooks Every Day*, by Melissa Hamilton and Christopher Hirsheimer. The chicory adds a pleasantly bitter note.

SERVES 4–6

For the tonnato sauce

1 small can (85–112g/3–4oz) of good tuna, preferably in olive oil

3–4 tablespoons good-quality mayonnaise

2 teaspoons capers, drained

2 teaspoons caper brine

1–2 canned anchovies, chopped

2 garlic cloves, peeled

1 tablespoon chopped fresh parsley, plus extra to garnish

a squeeze of lemon juice

sea salt and freshly ground black pepper

For the salad

as many juicy, ripe tomatoes as you like

chicory leaves, as you like

To make the tonnato sauce, whiz all its ingredients in a blender or food processor until smooth and well blended.

Arrange slices of tomato and the endive leaves on a lovely plate or platter. Pour over the sauce. Scatter with the extra parsley. Serve.

BAGNA CAUDA

An anchovy "bath" for a selection of vegetables and bread

The sheer simplicity of the ingredients here belies the silky-smooth "hot bath" they become, thanks to a little culinary alchemy. This recipe is adapted from the brilliant Marcella Hazan's *Classic Italian Cookbook*, and it is delicious. Like Ms Hazan, I like to serve it in a big pot at the centre of the table surrounded by vegetables, bread and multiple glasses of a robust Barbera . . .

SERVES 6-8

120ml (4fl oz) olive oil

40g (1½oz) unsalted butter

4 garlic cloves, finely chopped

2 x 55g (2oz) cans of anchovies, drained and snipped with scissors into small pieces

freshly ground black pepper

Heat the oil and butter in a saucepan until the butter is just about to foam. Turn down the heat and add the garlic. Cook a minute or two, but do not let it brown at all. Add the snipped anchovies and stir, cooking low and slow until the anchovies are dissolved. If it is still looking a little lumpy, use an immersion blender to whiz it all smooth.

Serve warm with crudités and bread.

PEPERONI RIPIENI

Baby peppers stuffed with anchovies and tomatoes

People forget the astonishing impact Delia Smith had upon British cooking in the 1980s. She included glycerine in one chocolate dessert, and it sold out . . . across the entire country. Seriously. Not an ounce was available. So I include this as an homage. In her *Summer Collection*, which appeared in 1989, Delia featured Peppers Piedmontese. My friends and I were just beginning to come around to the idea of inviting each other to dinner. We all cooked it. And loved it, and looked forward to it, and, and, and. This is it shrunk down to an *aperitivo*.

SERVES 4-6

300g (10½oz) sweet baby red peppers

55g (2oz) can of anchovies

12 cherry tomatoes, chopped

2 tablespoons capers, drained

3 garlic cloves, finely chopped

a handful of fresh basil, torn

olive oil, to drizzle

sea salt and freshly ground black pepper

Preheat the oven to 180°C (350°F), gas mark 4.

Split the peppers lengthways and gently remove the seeds. Place them in a baking tray or roasting tin.

Chop the anchovies and place a bit in each pepper cavity. Follow suit with the rest of the ingredients, finishing up by drizzling all of them with olive oil and seasoning with salt and pepper.

Pop them into the oven for 10–15 minutes, or until just cooked but not falling apart.

SCAMPI CON MAIONESE AL LIMONE E TIMO

Langoustines with lemon and thyme mayonnaise

Langoustines are madly popular across France, Spain and Italy. But as it turns out, most of them are caught in British waters. Why am I telling you this? Because, frankly, I want more of them in my life. And I don't necessarily want to travel to eat them. Fortunately, they are easy to cook.

SERVES 6

1kg (2lb 4oz) raw langoustines

sea salt

lemon wedges, to serve

For the mayonnaise

1–2 garlic cloves, peeled

a good pinch of sea salt

2 egg yolks

250ml (9fl oz) olive oil

a good squeeze of lemon juice

3–4 sprigs of fresh thyme, leaves only

freshly ground black pepper

First, cook the langoustines: bring a large stockpot of well-salted water to the boil. Add the langoustines and cook for about 7 minutes, or until cooked through. Then strain and set aside to cool.

Now make the mayonnaise: I like to make mine in a pestle and mortar (see page 89), but you can just as easily use a food processor. Just make sure the bowl is warm and dry before you begin. Blitz together the garlic and the salt. Add the egg yolks and pulse until they're well broken. Add the oil a little at a time, pulsing as you go, until you have the beginnings of your emulsion. Now, with the food processor on, add the remaining oil in a very gradual steady stream until it becomes a wobbly, creamy mayonnaise. Add the lemon juice and the thyme. Blitz again. Taste, and season with salt and pepper. Set aside.

(If you're not in the mood to make the mayonnaise – and let's face it, sometimes one simply isn't – spoon enough of a good-quality shop-bought mayonnaise into a bowl and stir in about half the quantity of thyme leaves, above.)

Serve the langoustines in a big bowl (with a spare one for the shells), with the mayonnaise and some lemon wedges on the side.

TIP: When you unroll a raw langoustine and look at its flesh through the soft under-shell, you will see that it's translucent. When it's cooked, it looks opaque.

OSTRICHE CON SALSA MIGNONETTE ALL' ITALIANA

Oysters with an Italian mignonette

My birthday happens to fall on the same day as the start of the British native oyster season. And one of my favourite birthday treats of all time involved setting off to West Mersea in Essex to eat these beauties straight out of the sea, washed down by lashings of white wine. It also helped that Jeremy Lee brought cake. Anyway, I got to thinking about an Italian-esque mignonette, and I thought this would do the job. It's bright and spicy, and balances nicely with the creaminess of a good oyster.

SERVES 4–6

1 dozen good oysters, shucked

For the mignonette

2 tablespoons finely chopped shallots

juice of 2 lemons

2 dried peperoncini, crumbled

1 teaspoon fresh oregano leaves, finely chopped

Tabasco, to serve (optional)

sea salt and freshly ground black pepper

Mix together all the ingredients for the mignonette in a small bowl. Leave to macerate for 10 minutes or so. Then serve alongside the freshly shucked oysters.

You can add a dab of Tabasco if you like.

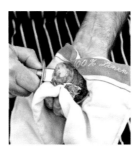

BOTTARGA SU PANE TOSTATO

Grated mullet roe on hot buttered toast

As with so many Italian recipes, this is the simplest of things, well in keeping with their philosophy of allowing a good ingredient to speak for itself. Here, the bottarga provides just the right amount of salty umami flavour to make your mouth water, and thus doubly allow you to appreciate that drink. Bottarga can be bought in the piece or grated into a fine powder, which is how I prefer to buy it. The Smeralda brand is readily available online and at good Italian delis.

MAKES 6-12

3 slices of good sourdough bread, toasted
unsalted butter
2–3 tablespoons grated cured mullet roe
freshly ground black pepper
lemon wedges, to serve (optional)

Butter the toast while it is still hot. Cut each slice into 2-4 pieces. Sprinkle the roe over the toast generously. Add pepper to taste.

Serve with lemon wedges, if you like.

CARPACCIO DI PESCE SPADA

Swordfish carpaccio

I used to eat plenty of swordfish carpaccio in Sicily, where it was freshly caught, sliced as thin as parchment and served with just a drizzle of olive oil, pepper, salt and lemon. I fear that I could never top that. But then I discovered that Forman & Field, in east London, make an air-dried cured swordfish carpaccio! It's utterly delicious and a simple and elegant antipasti option. If you can't find it (they have a wonderful online service), try smoked salmon or smoked trout instead.

SERVES 4-6

200g (7oz) air-dried swordfish carpaccio

½ red onion, finely sliced into rings

6–8 caper berries

2 tablespoons olive oil

a small handful of fresh flat-leaf parsley, leaves only

sea salt and freshly ground black pepper

lemon wedges, to serve

Lay the swordfish slices on a pretty plate. Top with the onion slices and the caper berries. Drizzle with the olive oil. Scatter over the parsley and season with salt and pepper.

Serve with lemon wedges on the side.

CAPELLINI CON GAMBERI GRIGI, AGLIO E CAPPERI

Capellini with brown shrimp, garlic and capers

Imagine the first Italians to visit Morecambe Bay in the north-west of England: what must they have thought of the glorious local shrimp? So sweet, so delicate, so damned delicious. This is a totally Br-Italian delight.

**SERVES 2 FOR LUNCH;
MAKES 6 COFFEE CUPS
SERVED AS *CICCHETTI***

150g (5½oz) capellini

4 tablespoons olive oil

2 garlic cloves, sliced

135g (4¾oz) brown shrimp

1 tablespoon capers, drained

zest of ½ lemon

a pinch of chopped fresh parsley

sea salt and freshly ground black pepper

Cook the pasta as per the instructions on the packet. But beware: capellini is so fine that it goes fast – keep your eyes on it, and check it frequently to ensure it doesn't go over.

Meanwhile, heat the oil in a saucepan and sauté the garlic until it's beginning to take colour. Add the brown shrimp, capers and lemon zest. Toss together. Turn off the heat and taste. Add salt, to taste, if necessary, and a good grinding of black pepper. Then add the drained pasta with a splash or two of its water. Toss together once more, adding the parsley, and serve.

MEAT & FOWL

CROCCHETTE ALLA 'NDUJA

Deep-fried croquettes flavoured with spicy 'nduja sausage

'Nduja is one of my favourite Italian ingredients. It is a soft spicy sausage from Calabria, the place where Italian food becomes seriously spicy. They *love* chillies there. And 'nduja is riddled with the little things. Note, however, that some 'ndujas are spicier than others . . .

MAKES 18–24

500g (1lb 2oz) floury potatoes (I favour King Edwards), peeled and chopped

2 tablespoons olive oil

55g (2oz) 'nduja sausage, peeled if in casing

a good squeeze of lemon juice

oil, for deep-frying

2 eggs, beaten

100g (3½oz) fine dried breadcrumbs

sea salt and freshly ground black pepper

Boil the potatoes in a large pan of lightly salted water until tender. Drain and mash well with the olive oil. When fairly smooth, add the 'nduja sausage meat and mash until you get a nice smooth, uniform texture. Add the lemon juice, salt and pepper and have a little taste. Adjust the seasoning to taste.

With clean hands, roll into small log shapes, placing them on a baking tray lined with nonstick baking paper as you go. Cover gently and place in the fridge until you are ready to cook.

Heat the oil to 180°C (350°F) in a deep fat fryer.

Meanwhile, take the "logs" out of the fridge. Dip them into the beaten eggs, then into the breadcrumbs, and deep-fry until crisp and golden. Drain on kitchen paper. Eat while they're still hot.

TARTARE DI VITELLO

Veal tartare and goats' cheese cream with grappa-marinated pears

This recipe comes from Appia, an Italian restaurant in Bangkok, run by my friend Jarrett Wrisley and his business partner Paolo Vitaletti. As soon as I read its description on their menu, I knew I had to get the recipe. It's sophisticated, decadent and very, very impressive.

SERVES 4-6

For the tartare

750g (1lb 10oz) veal fillet

3–4 anchovies, very finely chopped

½ tablespoon mustard

1 shallot, finely chopped

6–7 drops of Worcestershire sauce

a dash of balsamic vinegar

2 drops of Tabasco sauce

flat-leaf parsley, to garnish

For the goats' cheese cream

100g (3½oz) soft goats' cheese

50ml (2fl oz) double cream

For the pears

2 firm ripe pears

a good squeeze of lemon juice

25ml (1fl oz) grappa

For the salad

200g (7oz) wild rocket or mixed baby leaves

1–2 teaspoons balsamic vinegar

sea salt and freshly ground black pepper

Using a very sharp knife, chop the veal into about 3mm (⅛ inch) dice. Place it in a non-reactive bowl and add all the other tartare ingredients. Mix well and set aside.

Whisk the soft goats' cheese and the cream together until silky smooth.

Cut the pears into about 5mm (¼ inch) dice, keeping them under acidulated water as you go to prevent them turning brown. Toss the pear cubes in the grappa.

When ready to serve, toss the rocket or mixed leaves with the balsamic vinegar and season to taste with salt and pepper.

Plate the veal tartare and top with the goats' cheese cream. At Appia, they like to serve the tartare atop the salad. I like to serve it on the side, and to garnish the plate with flat-leaf parsley.

ROTOLI DI BRESAOLA CON ASPARAGI ARROSTO

Cured beef wrapped around spears of roasted asparagus

This plate of food combines two of my absolute favourite things – and it's such a doddle to make that you can spend more time sipping and chatting with pals.

MAKES 18-24

18–24 spears of asparagus, washed and trimmed

3–4 sprigs of fresh thyme

2 garlic cloves, bashed in their skins

2 tablespoons olive oil

18–24 slices of bresaola

sea salt and freshly ground black pepper

Preheat the oven to 200°C (400°F), gas mark 6.

Dry the asparagus thoroughly. Place it in a roasting tin along with the thyme, garlic and olive oil. Season with salt and pepper and toss so everything is well combined.

Pop the tin into the oven, giving it a gentle shake now and then, for 15–20 minutes, or until the asparagus is cooked through but still firm.

Remove from the oven and leave to cool a little. Once cool enough to handle, wrap a slice of bresaola around each spear and serve.

POLPETTE

Pork and herb meatballs with tomato sauce

I know that we commonly think of meatballs in the context of a pasta sauce, but Italian friends of mine have been serving them as *aperitivi* for years. Each meatball is a perfect savoury mouthful. Serve with bread, and try not to fight over who gets to wipe up the last vestiges of sauce.

MAKES 30–40

For the meatballs

200g (7oz) minced beef

200g (7oz) minced pork

200g (7oz) minced veal

2 garlic cloves, crushed

1 egg

3 tablespoons fresh breadcrumbs

2 tablespoons grated Parmesan cheese

½ tablespoon dried oregano

½ tablespoon chopped fresh flat-leaf parsley

salt and freshly ground black pepper

For the sauce

2 tablespoons olive oil

1 onion, finely chopped

2 garlic cloves, finely chopped

400g (14oz) can of tomatoes

500g (1lb 2oz) passata

1 tablespoon tomato purée

2 tablespoons dried oregano

125ml (4fl oz) white wine

75ml (2½fl oz) milk

First, make the meatballs. Place all the ingredients in a large bowl, and work together by hand until well combined. Then shape into balls (just smaller than a ping pong ball) and put in the fridge to rest for 30 minutes or so while you make the sauce.

Gently heat the olive oil in a deep frying pan or sauté pan, add the onion and cook until soft and translucent. Add the garlic and cook gently for another 5 minutes or so until fragrant. Don't let the garlic colour.

Add the tomatoes, passata and tomato purée, and season with salt, pepper and the oregano. Add the wine and the milk, stir the ingredients together and reduce to a good-looking sauce.

Now, with the sauce on the lowest possible simmer, add the meatballs. Cook them in the sauce for about 15 minutes, until they are cooked through.

Serve in bowls or on small plates, with a little extra black pepper and some bread on the side.

POLPETTE DI TACCHINO

Turkey meatballs

I think turkey is wildly underrated. Its critics say it's tasteless. I say it's a terrific vehicle for flavour. I also say that, if a roast turkey's tasteless, someone's not cooking it right and I will refer them to my recipe in *Leon: Family & Friends*. So there. These turkey meatballs are packed with herbs and, once they've cooled down a little, are perfect finger food.

MAKES ABOUT 28

3 tablespoons olive oil

150ml (5fl oz) white wine

juice of ½ lemon

25g (1oz) butter

chopped fresh parsley, to garnish

For the meatballs

500g (1lb 2oz) minced turkey

1 onion, finely chopped

2 garlic cloves, finely chopped

a good pinch of dried oregano

1 tablespoon chopped fresh parsley

2 sprigs of fresh thyme, leaves only

zest of ½ lemon

2 tablespoons fresh breadcrumbs

1 egg

sea salt and freshly ground black pepper

In a large bowl, mix all the meatball ingredients together by hand, then shape into balls about the size of a ping pong ball. Set the meatballs aside in the fridge for about 30 minutes or so before cooking.

Heat 2 tablespoons of the olive oil in a heavy-based frying pan, and cook the meatballs, in batches, all the way through, setting them aside on kitchen paper as you go. You may need the extra tablespoon of oil for the later meatballs, you may not.

Now deglaze the pan with the wine, scraping up the cooking residue into the sauce. When it has reduced by two-thirds, add the lemon juice and butter and stir into a glossy emulsion. Taste and adjust the seasoning. Return the meatballs to the pan and toss them through the sauce. Turn out on to a serving plate and garnish with the chopped parsley.

RISOTTO AL FEGATO DI POLLO E ROSMARINO

Risotto flavoured with rosemary and topped with sautéed chicken livers

This was inspired by a delicious plate of risotto I had at Enoteca Turi, a restaurant that used to be one of my locals in south-west London, but has now moved north of the river to Chelsea. The creamy, herby rice balances beautifully with the Marsala richness of the tender chicken livers.

SERVES 6–8 AS AN *APERITIVO*

For the risotto

1 litre (1¾ pints) chicken stock

1 tablespoon olive oil

25g (1oz) butter

1 shallot, chopped

1 garlic clove, chopped

1 teaspoon finely chopped fresh rosemary leaves

175g (6oz) risotto rice

100ml (3½fl oz) white wine

2 tablespoons grated Parmesan cheese, plus more to serve

sea salt and freshly ground pepper

chopped fresh parsley, to garnish

For the livers

1–2 tablespoons olive oil

25g (1oz) butter

300g (10½oz) chicken livers, trimmed

50ml (2fl oz) Marsala

Have the chicken stock simmering in a large pan within easy reach.

Heat the oil and butter in a heavy-based saucepan. Fry the shallot until softened slightly. Add the garlic and stir. Add the rosemary and stir through. Add the rice and stir until well coated. Add the white wine and stir well until absorbed.

Now add a ladle of the simmering stock and stir in until absorbed. Add another ladle, then carry on like this until you have a creamy risotto that still retains a little bite – it should take about 20 minutes. Just sip on a glass of wine while you're stirring!

Add the grated Parmesan and mix. Season with salt and pepper to taste. Cover with a lid and set aside to rest.

Heat a frying pan over a medium heat. Add the olive oil and butter. When hot, add the chicken livers and sauté until they are just done – you want them brown outside and slightly pink inside. Add the Marsala and bubble furiously for a couple of minutes until you have a syrupy sauce. Season with salt and pepper. Remove from the heat.

Serve the risotto in shallow bowls, with a liver or two atop each portion and some of the Marsala sauce drizzled over. Sprinkle over some parsley and serve extra Parmesan on the side.

FRED'S CARPACCIO

Seared beef fillet, sliced wafer thin

Traditionally carpaccio is made with raw beef; it's chilled, then very thinly sliced. But when Fred lived in Florence, renting a room off an elderly couple called the Cappellis, Signora Cappelli seared it, I think so that its rawness didn't upset the English boy! So Fred taught me this method and I love it. The sear forms a lovely crust and it has proved really popular with our friends too. If you want to be traditional, just roll your fillet tightly in clingfilm and pop it into the freezer for an hour. Slice it thinly, then put the slices between two pieces of baking paper and pound them with a rolling pin. Then proceed to serve, dressed as below.

SERVES 4–6

500g (1lb 2oz) beef fillet steak, in the piece

3 tablespoons olive oil

100g (3½oz) Parmesan cheese

a good handful of rocket

sea salt and freshly ground black pepper

lemon wedges, to serve

balsamic vinegar, to serve

Heat a nonstick griddle or frying pan over a high heat. Rub the beef fillet all over with 1 tablespoon of the olive oil and season it thoroughly with salt and pepper. Grill or pan-fry it for about 2–3 minutes on each side, so that it's seared on the outside, but still very rare. Set it aside on a plate to rest for 10–15 minutes, then put it into the fridge until it's completely cold. Roll tightly in clingfilm and pop it into the freezer for an hour.

When you are ready to serve, remove the beef from the freezer and slice it as thinly as possible, using a very sharp knife. Plate on to one main platter or individual plates. Drizzle the remaining olive oil over the beef and season again with salt and pepper. Shave the Parmesan over the beef and finish with the rocket.

Serve with lemon wedges and balsamic vinegar on the side.

ALETTE DI POLLO ALLA DIAVOLA

Devilled chicken wings

The devil made me do it . . . these wings are hot and spicy and – well, finger-licking good. You will need some cool drinks to douse the fire.

SERVES 6-8

1kg (2lb 4oz) chicken wings

For the marinade
3 tablespoons vegetable oil

½ teaspoon crushed dried chillies

½ tablespoon black peppercorns, cracked

½ tablespoon white peppercorns, cracked

1 tablespoon English mustard

1 sprig of fresh rosemary, leaves only

zest of 1 lemon

a good pinch of sea salt

Cut the chicken wings into their separate joints. Either keep the tips for stock or discard them. Place the middle sections and the wings' drummers in a large bowl. In a separate bowl, mix all the marinade ingredients together. Then pour this over the chicken and mix everything together thoroughly. Cover with clingfilm, and leave to marinate in the fridge for a good hour or two.

When you're ready to cook, preheat the oven to 200°C (400°F), gas mark 6. Lay the chicken pieces in a roasting tray and bake for about 30–40 minutes, turning once, until they are cooked through. They should be sticky and delicious.

ARANCINI SICILIANI

Deep-fried risotto balls filled with traditional Sicilian beef ragù

Just imagine large crispy-coated balls of hot rice packed with a surprise filling of rich, earthy beef ragù. Or alternatively, make these. Then you can move past the imagination part and go straight to the satisfaction. And what satisfaction they provide – if Mick and Keef had had the recipe, we'd be talking about a whole different song. Note that the ragù part of the recipe makes way more than you will need. But if one is going to go through the long, slow cooking that a great ragù needs, then why not make a big batch? Use the rest on pasta or freeze it for a rainy day.

MAKES ABOUT 8–12

For the ragù

1 onion

1 carrot

1 celery stick

2 garlic cloves

4 tablespoons olive oil

500g (1lb 2oz) minced beef

150ml (5fl oz) red wine

2 x 400g (14oz) cans of chopped tomatoes

1 bay leaf

1 tablespoon dried oregano

1 tablespoon tomato purée

75ml (2½fl oz) milk

sea salt and freshly ground black pepper

Make the ragù first. Chop the onion, carrot, celery and garlic roughly and then blitz them in a food processor or mini chopper.

Heat 2 tablespoons of the olive oil in a large pan. Add the chopped vegetables and fry them gently until they have softened. Remove from the heat. Scoop out the vegetables and set aside.

Wipe out the pan and add the remaining olive oil. Heat it over a medium heat and then crumble in the minced beef. Fry, stirring when necessary, until it is nicely browned. Now reintroduce the vegetables and give them a good stir. Add the red wine, bring to the boil and let it bubble for a couple of minutes, just to concentrate the flavour and cook out the alcohol. Now add the tomatoes, bay leaf, dried oregano, tomato purée and milk. Season with salt and pepper, and stir everything together. Bring back to the boil, then turn down to the lowest simmer you can.

Let it hum away merrily on the stovetop for 1–1½ hours. Taste and adjust the seasoning. If you still feel that the ragù is a little wet, just turn the heat up and bubble it a bit. Let the ragù cool completely, then refrigerate overnight.

RECIPE CONTINUES OVER THE PAGE

ARANCINI SICILIANI

For the rice

1.2 litres (2 pints) good chicken stock

1 tablespoon olive oil

20g (¾oz) butter, plus an extra knob

1 onion, finely chopped

2 garlic cloves, finely chopped

250g (9oz) risotto rice

100ml (3½fl oz) white wine

2–3 tablespoons freshly grated Parmesan cheese

sea salt and freshly ground black pepper

To make the arancini

50g (1¾oz) plain flour

2 eggs, beaten

125g (4½oz) fine breadcrumbs

vegetable oil, for deep-frying

To make the risotto, bring the stock to a gentle simmer in a large saucepan.

In a separate pan, heat the oil and butter over a low to medium heat. Add the onion and cook gently until it's translucent. Add the garlic and cook for another minute or so. Then add the rice, stirring it through the garlic and onion for a couple of minutes until it is well coated. Add the wine, turning up the heat and stirring the rice until almost all the wine has been absorbed. Now add a ladleful of stock. Stir the rice, cooking it over a medium heat until most of the stock has been absorbed, then add more stock, being careful not to flood the rice at any time, and cook until it has been absorbed again. Keep adding stock and absorbing it into the rice until it is cooked to the texture you like. You will probably have a little stock left over.

When the rice is done, season it with salt and pepper to taste. Then add the Parmesan and stir thoroughly through the rice. Add the extra knob of butter and stir through. Set the risotto aside until it's cold. Then refrigerate, covered, until you need it. You can make this up to 2 days before, if you want.

When ready to roll the arancini, prepare a three-stage "bread-crumbing" area: place the seasoned flour, the 2 beaten eggs, and the breadcrumbs in their own bowls in a row.

Take the risotto out of the fridge and, with cool hands (keep them cool and a little damp by running them under cold water), roll it into balls a bit smaller than a tennis ball. Flatten them slightly in your palm, and make a slight indent. Spoon some ragù into each one and roll them back into balls, enclosing the meat sauce. Now roll them first in the flour, shaking off the excess, then in the beaten egg, and finally in the breadcrumbs. Place all the balls on a baking tray lined with nonstick baking paper, and return them to the fridge until you're ready to cook.

Heat the oil to 180°C (350°F) in a deep-fat fryer. Once it is at temperature, cook the arancini a few at a time for about 3–4 minutes, or until crisp and golden brown. Drain briefly on kitchen paper and serve hot.

LA PANADA SARDA DI SUSANNA

Traditional Sardinian pies filled with lamb, peas and potatoes, from Susanna Mattana

When Susanna Mattana first made these pies for me, they were an absolute revelation. She is the chef-proprietor of the London-based Sardinian restaurant Isola del Sole, and her cooking is spectacular. Traditionally the pies are made with eel, but this lamb version is popular too, and it's much easier to find its ingredients. The origins of the dish seem to point to Spain, but it is the *cucina povera* of the region. Pre-refrigeration, the pies in their dense crisp pastry would keep for days. These are mini versions of the usually large pie.

MAKES 12–16

1kg (2lb 4oz) "00" flour, plus extra for dusting

150g (5½oz) lard

350g (12oz) lamb leg steaks, chopped

4–6 garlic cloves, chopped

25g (1oz) sun-dried tomatoes, chopped

200g (7oz) frozen peas

a good handful of fresh flat-leaf parsley, chopped

6 tablespoons olive oil, plus extra to top up the pies

sea salt

To make the pastry, put the flour, a dessertspoon of salt and the lard into a stand mixer with a dough hook. Mix until well combined, then start adding warm water a little at a time until you have a smooth dough, like a bread dough. Remove the pastry from the bowl of the mixer.

Very lightly flour a work surface – you really don't want to add any more flour to the dough if you can help it – and knead for 5 minutes, until silky and elastic. Wrap with clingfilm and set aside for about 30 minutes while you prepare the filling.

Put the lamb, garlic, sun-dried tomatoes, peas and parsley into a large bowl with the 6 tablespoons of olive oil. Mix all together well. Season with a little salt.

Very lightly flour a surface. Mark the pastry into 4 pieces. Keeping the pieces that are not being used wrapped in the clingfilm, roll out one piece at a time to about 5mm (¼ inch) thick. Then, using a roughly 15cm (6 inch) round template, maybe a glass or a bowl, start cutting out circles – you will get 3 or 4 out of each piece. Keep the trimmings close by to form the hats of the pies. Pile 2–3 heaped tablespoons of

RECIPE CONTINUES OVER THE PAGE

LA PANADA SARDA DI SUSANNA

the filling into the middle of each circle – we want plenty of filling, but we can add more in a bit.

Now for the fiddly bit: bring the edges of each circle up to form a cup shape, then, pleating the pastry together as you go, fold it around the filling. At this point you can see if you want to add more filling. Take small balls of the trimmings and roll them out to fit the tops of the pies, with some overlap. Now – and Susanna says this is very important – before fixing the tops on, you pour in enough olive oil to completely cover the filling. Fit the pastry lids on to the tops of the pie cases and squeeze the edges together to seal.

Trim any overlap with scissors, then twist and crimp the edges in a circular motion with your thumb and forefinger to finish each pie.

Repeat with the rest of the dough and filling.

Preheat the oven to 220°C (425°F), gas mark 7.

Place on a baking tray lined with nonstick baking paper and cook in the oven for about 30 minutes. Reduce the heat to 200°C (400°F), gas mark 6, and bake for a further 50–60 minutes, or until crisp and golden.

Serve hot from the oven.

COSTOLETTE DI AGNELLO

Tender lamb cutlets marinated in rosemary and thyme

I originally had this dish made with kid cutlets (that's baby goat, not baby people . . .). They have a wonderful earthy flavour, but they are so hard to find. Lamb is easier to get and tastes just as delicious. If you can source some kid cutlets, do give them a try. Ask the butcher to French trim the cutlets if he can – it makes for a nice "handle".

MAKES 8-12

4 tablespoons olive oil

4–6 garlic cloves, bashed in their skins

4–6 sprigs of fresh thyme

4–6 sprigs of fresh rosemary

8–12 lamb cutlets

sea salt and freshly ground black pepper

lemon wedges, to serve

Mix together the olive oil, garlic and herbs in a large bowl. Add the lamb and mix well to coat. Add a good grinding of black pepper and stir again. Then leave to marinate for at least an hour.

Heat a griddle pan until very hot.

Shake the excess oil off the lamb chops and season them with salt. Cook for about 2–3 minutes on each side, until the cutlets are well browned but still nicely pink inside. Leave to rest on a warm plate, then serve with wedges of lemon.

SPIEDINI DI PORCHETTA

Skewers of porchetta

Porchetta or pork belly stuffed with herbs and garlic, roasted long and slow and served in bread rolls slathered with salsa verde, is one of the great delights of a weekend in Florence. It is far too substantial to be called a snack. But I love those flavours. So here I have made a daintier version that still packs a punch.

SERVES 6 AS A SNACK

450g (1lb) pork leg steaks

1 tablespoon fennel seeds

2 sprigs of fresh rosemary, leaves only, chopped

4 tablespoons olive oil

1 garlic clove, crushed in its skin

1 dried peperoncino (optional)

sea salt and freshly ground black pepper

salsa verde (see page 144), to serve

Cut the pork steaks into bite-sized pieces.

Crush the fennel seeds and the rosemary leaves together in a pestle and mortar. Mix in the olive oil. Pour the mixture in a bowl, add the pork and stir to coat evenly. Cover and place in the fridge to marinate for 1–3 hours. Season with salt and pepper.

Heat a frying pan until hot, then add the pork with all the oil marinade. Cook, tossing the pork in the pan until golden and cooked through – about 6–8 minutes. Just before you take the pork out of the pan, add the crushed garlic and the peperoncino, if using, and stir it around – you want it to stick to the meat, but not to burn. Serve piping hot, with sticks or little forks for each guest and some salsa verde on the side.

LINGUA CON SALSA VERDE

Veal or ox tongue with herby green sauce

I have prepared tongue from scratch before now, but it is a long and rather gruesome process, so we won't go into it now. When I find I have a hankering for its sweet flavour and texture, I buy it from a good deli. It saves guests from the shock of opening the fridge and seeing a whole tongue lying there in all its glory . . .

SERVES 4–6

260g (9½oz) sliced cooked tongue

For the salsa verde

6 garlic cloves

55g (2oz) can of anchovies, drained

2 tablespoons capers, drained

a large handful of fresh basil

a large handful of fresh mint

a large handful of fresh flat-leaf parsley

juice of 1 lemon

a good dash of white wine vinegar

8 tablespoons olive oil, maybe more

freshly ground black pepper

Pop all the salsa verde ingredients into a food processor or mini chopper. Whiz them up, trying to retain a little texture.

Taste and adjust the seasoning. Serve draped over the tongue slices.

LINGUA CON SALSA VERDE

INSALATA DI ARANCIA E FINOCCHIO
see page 163

UOVA ALLA DIAVOLA CALABRESI

Calabrian devilled eggs

As mentioned earlier, the Calabrians are the kings and queens of Italian chillies. So it made perfect sense in my chilli-fevered imagination to make a devilled egg with their fiery 'nduja sausage. I hope they approve. And if not, so what? These feisty fellows make the perfect accompaniment to a frosty glass of Prosecco . . .

MAKES 12

4 slices of pancetta or prosciutto

6 large hard-boiled eggs, cooled and shelled

80g (2¾oz) good-quality 'nduja sausage, peeled if in casing

60ml (2¼fl oz) crème fraîche

2 tablespoons mayonnaise

sea salt and freshly ground black pepper

First, make the ham garnish. Preheat the oven to 180°C (350°F), gas mark 4. Lay the ham slices on a piece of foil. Fold the foil over the ham, then sandwich it tight between 2 baking trays. Pop into the oven for about 15 minutes. Remove the ham from the trays and the foil, and set aside on kitchen paper to drain and cool. Once cold, the slices of ham can be kept in an airtight container until needed.

Halve the hard-boiled eggs and gently scoop the yolks out into a clean bowl. Mash thoroughly with the 'nduja sausage, crème fraîche and mayonnaise. Taste, then season lightly with salt and pepper.

Scoop the yolk mixture back into the reserved egg whites and garnish each with a shard of crispy pancetta or prosciutto. Serve straight away.

VEGETABLES, DAIRY & EGGS

PANZANELLA

Tuscan bread and tomato salad

Another rustic, simple dish that, when put together using good ingredients, becomes a stunner. Traditionally, it was made to use up leftover stale bread, but I prefer using lightly toasted chunks, to keep some texture.

SERVES 6

1 orange or red pepper

150g (5½oz) crusty white bread, lightly toasted and torn into chunks

6–8 ripe, juicy tomatoes, halved or quartered

1 small cucumber, halved lengthways, deseeded and sliced

1 red onion, sliced

60ml (2¼fl oz) red wine vinegar

60ml (2¼fl oz) extra virgin olive oil

a good pinch of fresh oregano

a handful of fresh basil leaves

1 tablespoon capers, drained (optional)

sea salt and freshly ground black pepper

Holding it with tongs, blister the pepper over the gas flame of your cooker until blackened. If you don't cook on gas, you can char it under a hot grill. Pop the charred pepper into a plastic bag to sweat – this will make peeling it easier.

Meanwhile, toss together the bread, tomatoes, cucumber and red onion in a large bowl.

Peel and deseed the pepper, then dice. Add to the salad.

Make a dressing by whisking the vinegar, olive oil, oregano, salt and pepper together. Pour over the salad – you may not need all of it. Mix gently, adding the basil and the capers, if using. Traditionally, you would allow this salad to macerate for 30 minutes or so, but I like to serve it straight away.

"PATATINE FRITTE" DI POLENTA AL ROSMARINO

Polenta "fries" with rosemary and sea salt

When I had the great pleasure of co-writing *The Tucci Table* with the ever-charming actor Stanley Tucci and his wife Felicity Blunt, this was one of the stars of the show. Crisp, hot polenta "fries" with a herby salt. I have changed a couple of things, but otherwise, why mess with perfection? As an alternative to the herbs in the salt, try a few shavings of truffle . . .

SERVES 4–6

200g (7oz) cooked polenta, chilled

120g (4¼oz) Parmesan cheese, freshly grated

oil, for deep-frying

2 sprigs of fresh rosemary, leaves only, chopped

4 sprigs of fresh thyme, leaves only

sea salt and freshly ground black pepper

Slice the cold polenta into finger-sized sticks. Gently roll each one in the grated Parmesan. Pop them on to a sheet of nonstick baking paper on a baking tray. If the weather is hot, place them in the fridge until needed.

Heat the oil to 180°C (350°F) in a deep-fat fryer. Fry the polenta sticks in batches until crisp and golden. This should take about 3–4 minutes per batch. Remove and drain on kitchen paper. Then, while still hot, season with sea salt, pepper, fresh rosemary and thyme, and serve at once.

SPAGHETTI CON OLIO, AGLIO E VINO ROSSO

Spaghetti cooked with red wine, oil and garlic

Is this an *aperitivo* dish? Probably not. It's probably the perfect pasta to serve before Bistecca Fiorentina. And it's beautiful. And I like to smuggle a few main dishes into this book . . . I also think this dish demonstrates one of my favourite things about Italian food – its brilliant simplicity. I first had it at a restaurant on the Via dei Benci in Florence. I thought I had it figured out, but I could never get the final step of the emulsion. I don't know why, but it never occurred to me to finish the pasta in the sauté pan. So many thanks to my splendid chum Pepe Mallardo for telling me. Two things, though. First, you need to know how long your spaghetti takes to cook. Every brand I've ever used reaches a perfect *al dente* before the time suggested on the packet. You pull the pasta out of its water early here to finish it with the garlic. Second, you only use 600ml (21fl oz) of wine in all. The other 150ml (5fl oz) I like to call cook's perks.

**SERVES 2 AS A STARTER,
6 AS A SMALL *APERITIVO* SNACK**

1 bottle of red wine

200g (7oz) spaghetti

60ml (2¼fl oz) olive oil

2 garlic cloves, sliced lengthways

1 tablespoon chopped fresh parsley

sea salt and freshly ground black pepper

Pour 500ml (18fl oz) of red wine into a large saucepan, then top up with water. Season generously with salt and bring to the boil. Add the spaghetti and cook until it's about 2 minutes away from your preferred *al dente* texture.

Meanwhile, heat the olive oil in a sauté pan and gently poach the garlic.

When the pasta has reached that not-quite-done moment, add 100ml (3½fl oz) of red wine to the garlic and oil, whack up the heat and, with tongs, add the pasta to the garlic.

Cook the pasta until the wine emulsion has reduced to a syrupy texture. Remove from the heat, season with salt and pepper, and stir in the parsley.

Serve at once.

ZUPPA DI POMODORO CON ORIGANO E TIMO

Tomato soup with oregano and thyme

Soup for an *aperitivo*, you say? Why not. Served hot in winter or chilled in the summer, this delicious tomato soup is simplicity itself.

MAKES 8 SMALL SERVINGS

2 tablespoons olive oil

1 onion, finely chopped

2–3 garlic cloves, finely chopped

3–4 sprigs of fresh thyme, leaves only

3–4 sprigs of fresh oregano, leaves only, plus extra to garnish

100ml (3½fl oz) white wine

2 x 400g (14oz) cans of chopped tomatoes

100ml (3½fl oz) vegetable stock

sea salt and freshly ground black pepper

Frico del Friuli (see page 175), to serve (optional)

Heat the oil in a saucepan over a medium heat. Add the onion and cook until slightly softened. Add the garlic and the herbs and stir for another minute. Add the white wine and give it a bubble. Add the tomatoes and the stock. Bring back to the boil and simmer gently for 4–5 minutes.

Carefully pour the soup into a blender or food processor and blitz until smooth. Pour back into the pan and season with salt and pepper to taste. Top each portion with an oregano leaf and serve straight away, with some Frico del Friuli on the side, if desired, or chill until icy.

SUPPLÌ AL TELEFONO CON PORCINI E TARTUFO

Deep-fried balls of porcini mushroom and truffle risotto with a gooey mozzarella centre

What can I say about these morsels that hasn't already been uttered? Crisp, fragrant, with the "telephone wire" of oozing mozzarella in the middle. Pour me a crisp Prosecco and hand me a plateful . . .

MAKES ABOUT 24

30g (1oz) dried porcini mushrooms
600ml (20fl oz) hot water
600ml (20fl oz) vegetable stock
1 tablespoon olive oil
20g (¾oz) butter, plus an extra knob
1 onion, finely chopped
2 garlic cloves, finely chopped
250g (9oz) risotto rice
100ml (3½fl oz) white wine
2–3 tablespoons freshly grated Parmesan cheese
1 tablespoon finely chopped fresh parsley
1 teaspoon good-quality truffle oil
50g (1¾oz) plain flour
2 eggs, beaten
125g (4½oz) fine dried breadcrumbs
75g (2¾oz) mozzarella cheese, chopped into about 24 pieces
vegetable oil, for deep-frying
sea salt and freshly ground black pepper

Place the porcini mushrooms in a deep bowl with the hot water and leave to soak for 1 hour. Drain, reserving the liquid, and squeeze any residual juices out of the mushrooms into the reserved liquid. Strain the liquid to filter out any bits of dirt. Chop the mushrooms into smallish pieces and set aside.

In a large saucepan, bring the stock and the porcini soaking water to a gentle simmer.

In a separate pan, heat the oil and butter over a low to medium heat. Add the onion and cook gently until it's translucent. Add the garlic and cook for another minute or so. Then add the rice, stirring it through the garlic and onion for a couple of minutes until it is well coated. Add the porcini mushrooms and stir to coat well. Add the wine, turning up the heat and stirring the rice until almost all the wine has been absorbed.

Now add a ladleful of stock. Stir the rice, cooking it over a medium heat until most of the stock has been absorbed, than add more stock, being careful not to flood the rice at any time, and cook until it has been absorbed again. Keep adding stock and absorbing it into the rice until it is cooked to the texture you like. You will probably have a little stock left over.

RECIPE CONTINUES OVER THE PAGE

SUPPLÌ AL TELEFONO CON PORCINI E TARTUFO

When the rice is done, season it with salt and pepper to taste. Then add the Parmesan, truffle oil and parsley and stir them thoroughly through the rice. Add the extra knob of butter and stir through. Set the risotto aside until it's cold. Then refrigerate it, covered, until you need it. You can make this up to 2 days before, if you want.

When ready to roll the *supplì*, prepare a three-stage "bread-crumbing" area: place the seasoned flour, the beaten eggs and the breadcrumbs in their own bowls in a row.

Take the risotto out of the fridge and, with cool hands (keep them cool and a little damp by running them under cold water), roll it into balls about the size of a large walnut. Flatten them slightly in your palm and push a piece of mozzarella into each one. Then roll them back into balls, enclosing the cheese. Now roll them in the flour, shaking off any excess, then in the beaten eggs, and finally in the breadcrumbs. Place all the balls on a baking tray lined with nonstick baking paper, and return them to the fridge until you're ready to cook.

Heat the oil to 180°C (350°F) in a deep-fat fryer. Once it is at temperature, cook the *supplì* a few at a time for about 2–3 minutes, or until crisp and golden brown. Drain on kitchen paper and serve hot.

RISI E BISI

Rice and green peas

This warming Venetian dish is somewhere between a soup and a risotto – neither quite one nor the other, but beautiful in its own right. Serve in a large bowl and let everyone scoop some on to their plates or into cups.

SERVES 4-6

1 litre (1¾ pints) vegetable stock

1 tablespoon olive oil

40g (1½oz) butter, plus an extra knob

1 onion, finely chopped

1 garlic clove, finely chopped

175g (6oz) risotto rice

100ml (3½fl oz) white wine

350g (12oz) frozen peas

2–3 tablespoons grated Parmesan cheese

1 tablespoon fresh flat-leaf parsley, chopped

sea salt and freshly ground black pepper

SEE PAGE 62 FOR A PHOTOGRAPH OF THIS RECIPE

Bring the stock to the boil, then turn down to a simmer. Keep close to hand.

Heat the oil and butter in a heavy-based saucepan. Fry the onion until softened. Add the garlic and stir. Add the rice and stir until well coated. Add the white wine and stir and bubble well until absorbed.

Now add a ladle of the simmering stock and stir in until absorbed. Add the rest of the stock and the peas. Bring to the boil. Turn down to a simmer and let it cook for about 10–15 minutes. You want cooked rice, but more liquid than you would have with a risotto. Stir in the Parmesan, parsley and extra butter. Season with salt and pepper.

INSALATA DI TOPINAMBUR CON PECORINO

Jerusalem artichoke salad with Pecorino

I love the contrast of the earthy artichokes with the sharp cheese and tart dressing.

SERVES 6-8

400g (14oz) Jerusalem artichokes, washed and sliced very finely on a mandolin

200g (7oz) rocket

3 tablespoons extra virgin olive oil

2 tablespoons lemon juice

100g (3½oz) Pecorino cheese

sea salt and freshly ground black pepper

Toss the artichokes and the rocket together. Make a dressing by whisking the olive oil and lemon juice together and seasoning with salt and pepper to taste.

Dress the salad, tossing gently again. Shave over the Pecorino, using a cheese slice. Serve.

INSALATA DI ARANCIA E FINOCCHIO

Orange and fennel salad

This chic and simple salad is refreshingly bright, with a hit of citrus and the herbal notes of fennel. I often feel that this tastes like a Negroni on a plate . . .

SERVES 4-6

2–3 oranges – if you can get blood oranges, all the better
1–2 bulbs of fennel, trimmed
¼ red onion, thinly sliced into rings
2–3 tablespoons extra virgin olive oil
sea salt and freshly ground black pepper

SEE PAGE 145 FOR A PHOTOGRAPH OF THIS RECIPE

Peel and thinly slice the oranges, removing as much pith as possible, and reserve any juice.

Thinly slice the fennel.

Gently layer the fennel and orange slices on a plate, pouring over any juice that has come out of the oranges.

Scatter the onion slices over the top. Drizzle with olive oil and season with salt and pepper.

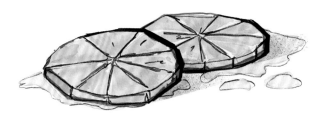

SALSA DI FAGIOLI TOSCANI

Tuscan bean dip

Super quick and easy, this can be made from pretty much what is in your cupboards and fridge. I always tend to have a few cans of beans lurking in my kitchen.

MAKES ABOUT 800G (1LB 12OZ)

2 x 400g (14oz) cans of cannellini beans, drained and rinsed

2 tablespoons extra virgin olive oil

1 shallot, chopped

2 garlic cloves, chopped

1 sprig of fresh rosemary, leaves only, finely chopped

a handful of fresh parsley, finely chopped

150ml (5fl oz) good chicken stock

sea salt and freshly ground black pepper

Pop everything bar the stock into a blender or food processor. Whiz up and add the chicken stock as you're whizzing – you may not need all of it. You want a nice creamy consistency. Add salt and pepper to taste.

Serve with crudités, breadsticks or crusty bread.

INSALATA PANTESCA

Pantellerian potato salad

Many years ago on a sailing trip from Malta to Sicily we took a detour and spent a couple of days and nights on the beautiful island of Pantelleria, where we ate the freshest grilled fish and many vegetable sides, all studded with copious local capers. This is a version of a fresh and light potato salad we had that remains to this day the tastiest I have ever had. (I would also add that my favourite *vin santo*, the honey-kissed Passito di Pantelleria, comes from this stunning isle . . .)

SERVES 4–6

500g (1lb 2oz) new potatoes

250g (9oz) cherry tomatoes

1 red onion, chopped or sliced – it's up to you

2–3 sprigs of fresh oregano, leaves only

3 tablespoons capers, drained

2 tablespoons good extra virgin olive oil

a good dash of red wine vinegar

sea salt and freshly ground black pepper

Bring the potatoes to the boil in a large pan of salted water. Cook until just done, then drain and refresh under cold running water to stop them cooking further.

Halve or quarter the cherry tomatoes and mix gently with the red onion, oregano and capers. Add the potatoes, halved or quartered if you like, and mix through. Add the oil, vinegar, salt and pepper. Taste and adjust.

Serve alongside some grilled meat or fish.

MOZZARELLA IN CARROZZA

Mozzarella cheese "in a carriage"

Let's be honest here, what could be more enticing than golden, crisp, lightly fried bread, oozing with gooey, melted mozzarella? Not much, that's what. All hail what is, in essence, an Italian toasted cheese sandwich. Just thinking about these makes me hungry.

MAKES 4-8

125g (4½oz) mozzarella cheese, sliced

4 slices of packaged soft white bread

2 tablespoons olive oil

50g (1¾oz) butter

sea salt and freshly ground black pepper

Divide the sliced mozzarella between 2 slices of the bread. Season with salt and pepper. Top with the remaining slices of bread and squeeze down lightly.

In a large frying pan, heat the oil and melt the butter. Once it is bubbling a little, pop the sandwiches in, one at a time if you need to. Fry until crisp and golden on both sides – gently turning once or twice.

Cut into 4 or 8 and serve straight away, with plenty of napkins.

TIP: Add a few torn leaves of fresh basil to the cheese if you like.

INSALATA CAPRESE

Bocconcini (tiny balls of mozzarella), cherry tomato and basil salad

This is a shrunken version of the classic salad. And it's rather more casual, as you can see. The quality of the ingredients is paramount here: do not skimp on getting the very best buffalo mozzarella you can, ripe tomatoes and fresh basil. It just doesn't work with lacklustre produce. But with the good stuff, it has all the flavour and the colours of the Italian flag!

SERVES 4-6

200g (7oz) cherry tomatoes, halved

250g (9oz) bocconcini (miniature mozzarella cheeses)

2–3 tablespoons extra virgin olive oil

a handful of fresh basil leaves

sea salt and freshly ground black pepper

crusty bread, to serve

Grab a beautiful bowl. Into it tumble the halved tomatoes, the bocconcini, torn if you like, and the olive oil. Season with salt and pepper, and toss in some roughly torn basil.

Serve with crusty bread.

FOGLIE DI SALVIA FRITTE

Deep-fried sage leaves

These are so, so elegant to serve with *aperitivi*. They provide that extra punch of flavour and texture to enhance everything else around them.

SERVES 4–6 AS A CONDIMENT

oil, for deep-frying

40g (1½oz) plain flour

10g (¼oz) cornflour

250ml (9fl oz) cold sparkling water

a large bunch of good fresh sage leaves, separated

Heat the oil to 180°C (350°F) in a deep-fat fryer.

Sift the flour and cornflour into a bowl and whisk in the sparkling water – you won't need all of it, just enough to make a batter the consistency of single cream.

Dip the sage leaves into the batter and carefully pop them straight into the hot oil. Fry for 2–3 minutes, or until blond and crisp. Drain each batch on kitchen paper, then transfer to a plate. Serve straight away.

FRICO DEL FRIULI

Crisp cheese discs

Typically this is made as one large circle or square in the Friuli region. I have made smaller versions here, all the easier to eat daintily while you sip a glass of chilled Refosco.

MAKES 24

250g (9oz) Parmesan cheese, grated finely

finely grated zest of ½ lemon

a good grinding of black pepper

Preheat the oven to 180°C (350°F), gas mark 4.

Mix all the ingredients gently together in a bowl until they're well combined.

Line 2 baking trays with silicone paper to prevent the fricos sticking, or use 1 tray and bake in 2 batches. If you only have nonstick baking paper, make sure you grease it. Then measure out 24 heaped tablespoons of the cheese and spread them out a few centimetres apart.

Bake them in the oven for about 4–6 minutes, until golden and melted. Be careful not to burn them.

Remove the Parmesan crisps from the oven. Leave them to cool a little, then take them off the silicone with a fish slice or a spatula and place them on a wire rack to cool. Set aside until needed, or store in an airtight container overnight.

FAGIOLI ALLA MALTESE

A Maltese–Italian dish of butter beans, garlic, parsley and olive oil

Okay, okay, so this is not Italian . . . but . . . when I was growing up, I spent a lot of time on the islands of Malta and Gozo, in the Mediterranean sea. And this was one of our all-time favourite things to eat with drinks in the evening – Maltese *aperitivi*, as it were. If you are in a real hurry, you can use canned or jarred beans. But if you cook them and serve them warm, it's heavenly.

SERVES 6-8

400g (14oz) dried butter beans, soaked overnight in cold water

2–3 garlic cloves, crushed

a handful of fresh parsley, chopped

2–3 tablespoons extra virgin olive oil

sea salt and freshly ground black pepper

Drain the soaked beans and rinse them under cold running water to get rid of any dirt or pebbles. Pop them into a clean saucepan and cover with plenty of water. Bring to the boil, skimming off any scum or froth that comes to the surface. Turn down to a simmer and pop the lid on until they are done – this could take 1–1½ hours. Drain and leave to cool a little.

If you're using canned or jarred beans (the big Spanish *judión* beans are fabulous), just drain and rinse them. Then proceed as follows.

Place the beans in a serving bowl. Stir in the garlic, parsley, olive oil, salt and pepper. Taste and add more of anything you like. Serve warm or at room temperature, with cocktail sticks.

BUCCE DI MELANZANA MARINATE AL PEPE

Pepe's quick-pickled aubergine skins

My local Italian deli, Giuliano's, is run by the charming Pepe Mallardo and his wife. One day I was marvelling at a new type of pickle on the side of my prosciutto sandwich, and I asked what this unusual vegetable was . . . and he informed me that it was pickled aubergine skin! Pepe never throws anything away, and now, nor do I. These are perfect alongside cold cuts, cheese or a frittata.

SERVES 4–6 AS A CONDIMENT

the peel from 1 large aubergine

2–3 tablespoons red wine vinegar

1 garlic clove, finely chopped

1 tablespoon chopped fresh parsley

sea salt and freshly ground black pepper

Blanch the aubergine peel for 1 minute in a large pan of boiling water, then plunge it straight into iced water. Strain the peel and dry it on kitchen paper.

Pop the peel into a non-reactive bowl and add the red wine vinegar, garlic, parsley, salt and pepper. Stir gently.

CAPONATA SICILIANA

Sicilian aubergine ragù

This was a dish that I craved every time we sailed to Sicily on my dad's boat. I'd order it straight away as a side to freshly grilled swordfish. But I soon discovered it was just as good at room temperature with crusty bread, as a snack.

SERVES 6-8

3–4 tablespoons olive oil

1 aubergine, cut into rough dice

1 small red onion, chopped

1 red pepper, deseeded and roughly chopped

1 red chilli, deseeded and chopped

2 celery sticks, chopped

10 cherry tomatoes, halved

1 tablespoon capers, drained

2 tablespoons sultanas

1 tablespoon sugar

3 tablespoons red wine vinegar

1 tablespoon pine nuts, toasted

8 pitted black olives, halved

1 tablespoon chopped fresh parsley

½ tablespoon extra virgin olive oil

sea salt and freshly ground black pepper

Heat 1 tablespoon of the olive oil in a frying pan. Add the aubergine and cook until golden brown on the cut sides. You may have to do this in batches so that you don't crowd the pan, and you may have to add a dash more oil as you go. Drain on kitchen paper.

Add another tablespoon of olive oil to the pan and cook the onion until it takes just a little colour. Then add the red pepper, chilli and celery, and stir together until nicely coated with the oil. Then return the aubergine to the pan and add the tomatoes. Stir through, then add the capers and sultanas.

Now mix together the sugar and the vinegar, add to the pan, cover and simmer for about 7 minutes. Remove the lid and cook for another 5 minutes or so, then remove from the heat and season with salt and pepper to taste.

Once the caponata has cooled to room temperature, add the pine nuts, olives and parsley, and dress with the extra virgin olive oil. Stir together gently and serve with crusty bread.

INSALATA PERE E GORGONZOLA

Pear and Gorgonzola salad

Sweet pears and strong, sharp, creamy Gorgonzola are a match made in heaven. The rocket adds a peppery note to cut against the cheese.

SERVES 4

a large handful of rocket

1–2 ripe but firm pears

a good squeeze of lemon juice

40g (1½oz) Gorgonzola cheese

1 tablespoon toasted pine nuts

2 tablespoons extra virgin olive oil

sea salt and freshly ground black pepper

Scatter the rocket over a pretty plate.

Slice the pears thinly while keeping their shape intact, from the stem down. Pop them into acidulated water as you go, to prevent them browning.

Shake any excess water off the pears and place them on top of the rocket. Scatter over the Gorgonzola and pine nuts. Finish by drizzling olive oil over the top and seasoning with a little salt and pepper.

FUNGHI SALTATI

Sautéed mushrooms

Earthy mushrooms, plenty of garlic, the spike of fresh lemon juice and bright basil. Serve with plenty of toasted bread.

SERVES 4-6

500g (1lb 2oz) mixed mushrooms – I used pied de mouton, shiitake and chestnut mushrooms

3 tablespoons olive oil

1 red onion, finely chopped

1 garlic clove, bashed in its skin

2–3 fresh red chillies, thinly sliced (optional)

a squeeze of lemon juice

a handful of fresh flat-leaf parsley, roughly torn

sea salt and freshly ground black pepper

Clean the mushrooms gently and chop into even-sized pieces.

Heat the oil in a large pan over a medium heat. Now bundle in the onion and the mushrooms at the same time. This may sound unconventional – but it works. Stir every now and then, and as the mushrooms release their liquid the onion will soften. This will take about 3–4 minutes.

Now add the garlic, and the chillies, if you're using them, and stir for another minute or so. Season with a squeeze of lemon juice and some salt and pepper. Remove from the heat and toss with some fresh basil, saving a little for later. Leave to cool to room temperature before serving. Scatter with the rest of the basil and serve with crusty bread.

SEDANO RAPA, RAVANELLI, INDIVIA E NOCI

Celeriac, Radish, Chicory and Walnut

Crunch, crunch, crunch: that's what this salad says. But with an Italian accent. It gives a lovely mouthful of texture and flavour with each bite . . .

SERVES 4

2 heads of chicory – try to get 1 red and 1 green, if you can

3 tablespoons olive oil

2 tablespoons white balsamic vinegar

120g (4¼oz) peeled celeriac, cut into matchsticks

4 radishes or 1 watermelon radish, cut into matchsticks

8 walnuts, crumbled

25g (1oz) Parmesan cheese, shaved

sea salt and freshly ground black pepper

Separate the chicory leaves and arrange on a serving plate. Mix together the oil and vinegar in a bowl and season with a little salt and pepper. Tumble the celeriac and the radish slices in the dressing, reserving a little of it, and pile on to the chicory.

Scatter the walnuts on top, along with the Parmesan shavings. Finish with the last drizzle of dressing and a little extra salt and pepper.

FAVE E FORMAGGIO

Fresh podded broad beans with sharp cheese

This is the most magical and utterly simple idea ever, and I have no shame in saying I have stolen it directly from the wonderful Rachel Roddy's book *Five Quarters*, on the food of Rome. Making this, I feel, should be a group activity – the podding of the beans, the breaking of the bread, the cutting of the cheese. Just make sure you accompany the job with a dry wine from the Marche, or a small Sbagliato . . .

SERVES 4–8

750g (1lb 10oz) broad beans, in their pods

300g (10½oz) good sharp cheese – Parmesan, Pecorino, Manchego, or even mature Cheddar

crusty bread, to serve

Gather your loved ones and start podding and skinning the beans, cutting chunks of cheese and tearing bread. Laugh, drink, eat. This is the *dolce vita*.

FRITTATA DI ERBE E FORMAGGIO

Herb and cheese frittata

An Italian frittata has more in common with a Spanish tortilla than it does a French omelette. They are cooked on both sides, slowly, until firm. Allegedly, some people flip their *frittate* like pancakes. I think this is a recipe for disaster, and ends with egg all over the floor and a very happy dog; the best solution is to finish the top gently under the grill (how I miss an old-fashioned, eye-level grill), or to turn them with the aid of a separate lid or plate in the modern Spanish style.

SERVES 4–6 AS AN *APERITIVO*

4 eggs

3 tablespoons grated Parmesan cheese

1 tablespoon torn fresh basil

1 tablespoon chopped fresh parsley

1 tablespoon chopped fresh oregano leaves

25g (1oz) butter

sea salt and freshly ground black pepper

Beat the eggs in a bowl until well combined, then add the cheese, herbs, salt and pepper, and beat again.

Melt the butter in a small but sturdy 16cm (6¼ inch) frying pan and, when it's foaming, add the egg mixture, turning down the heat to its lowest setting. Cook very gently until only the top of the frittata is still runny. Now either turn carefully with the aid of a lid and slide the frittata back into the pan to cook for another 45 seconds or so, or finish under the grill until just set.

Turn out on to a warm plate, cut into wedges, and serve.

BREAD & BAKING

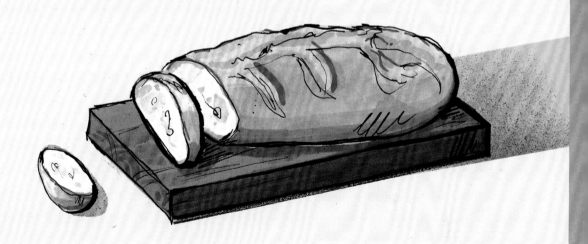

FOCACCIA CON OLIVE E ROSMARINO
Focaccia with Olives and Rosemary

I had the great pleasure of meeting *Great British Bake Off* finalist Richard Burr over an excellent cooked breakfast at the Pen-y-Dre B&B before the Abergavenny Food Festival. He was there to demo his doughs; I was there with enough sherry to inebriate at least half of Wales; naturally we got to asking each other what we were doing next. Which, for me, was this. "Got a focaccia recipe?" says I. "Sure," says he. And here it is. This recipe appears in his brilliant book *BIY: Bake It Yourself*.

MAKES 2 LOAVES

500g (1lb 2oz) strong white bread flour

2 teaspoons salt

1 tablespoon fast-action dried yeast

50ml (2fl oz) olive oil, plus extra for kneading, shaping and drizzling

350ml (12fl oz) water

20 pitted green olives, halved

a few sprigs of fresh rosemary, leaves only

sea salt and freshly ground black pepper

Put the flour into a bowl and add the salt and the yeast on opposite sides from each other, then stir together with a wooden spoon. Add the oil and water, and bring together into a wet dough.

Pour 2 tablespoons of olive oil on to your work surface and knead the dough on it for a good 10 minutes. You might need to add more flour, but this is supposed to be a wet dough – prepare to get a little oily.

Place the dough in an oiled plastic container that holds at least 2 litres (3½ pints), cover with clingfilm, and leave to prove until doubled in size.

Now turn out the dough on to an oiled work surface and cut it in half. Richard's tip is to oil the blades of 2 long knives. Use one to cut the dough, then slide the other in alongside it to push the 2 halves apart. Gently place each half on its own nonstick-paper-lined baking tray. Form each one into a lozenge shape, cover with plastic bags and leave to prove for another 45 minutes. Don't let the plastic touch the dough.

Preheat the oven to 220°C (425°F), gas mark 7, and uncover the dough.

Press the olive halves firmly into the dough, scatter with the rosemary leaves, drizzle with olive oil and season with salt and pepper.

Bake in the oven for 20–25 minutes, until golden, then leave to cool on wire racks. Finally, drizzle with more olive oil before cutting and . . . devouring.

TARALLI PUGLIESI

Puglian taralli biscuits

While *aperitivo* is very much a northern concept, it doesn't mean that they don't make delicious drinking snacks in the south. Like *taralli*, which I first discovered on my honeymoon, when we stayed at the beautiful Masseria Il Frantoio, run by Signor e Signora Ballastrazzi. (La Signora is one of the most extraordinary cooks I've ever met, cooking amazing fourteen-course banquets for the guests, and with a deep knowledge of Puglia's culinary history.) Every evening, before heading out for dinner, we'd enjoy a glass or two of white wine in the sun-dappled courtyard, served with fat green olives and La Signora's *taralli*. This recipe isn't hers exactly, but it's based on how she told me to make them.

MAKES ABOUT 18–22

250g (9oz) "00" flour, plus extra for dusting

a good pinch of salt

75ml (2½fl oz) extra virgin olive oil

100ml (3½fl oz) white wine

1½ teaspoons fennel seeds

Mix together the flour and salt in a bowl and add the liquids. Bring everything together into a dough, then turn out on to a floured surface and knead for 5 minutes. Add the fennel seeds, and knead again to spread them evenly through the dough. Return the dough to a clean bowl and set aside to rest for 30 minutes or so, covered with a cloth.

When you're ready to make the *taralli*, break the dough into walnut-sized pieces. Then roll each piece out into a rope that's about 4cm (1½ inches) long and 1cm (½ inch) in diameter. Shape each one into a rough circle, crossing and gently pinching the ends together.

Bring a large saucepan of water to the boil and, in batches, add the *taralli*. Cook until they float to the surface (just under a minute or so), then scoop out with a slotted spoon and set aside to dry and cool.

Preheat the oven to 190°C (375°F), gas mark 5. Place the *taralli* on baking trays and bake until golden and crunchy – about 35 minutes. Cool on wire racks and store in an airtight container until needed. They will keep for 3–5 days.

PANE ALLE OLIVE DI SUSANNA

Susanna Matanna's olive bread

My friend Susanna is one of the best bakers I know, and she makes these rolls fresh every day. If you get to her restaurant for an early lunch, they are served warm, fresh from the oven. Which is a jolly good incentive to be there when they open the doors . . . In the interests of full disclosure, I should probably tell you that I borrowed a couple of loaves as a prop for the book's photo shoot. Our little team – Juliette, Tamin and Steph – devoured them as soon as we'd got the shot, and demanded I include the recipe. Fortunately for all, Susanna was happy to oblige.

MAKES 4 SMALL LOAVES

1 teaspoon sugar

350ml (12fl oz) warm water

20g (¾oz) fresh yeast or 10g (¼oz) dried active yeast

3 tablespoons extra virgin olive oil

1kg (2lb 4oz) strong white bread flour or "00" flour, plus extra for dusting

25g (1oz) pitted green olives, chopped

25g (1oz) pitted black olives, chopped

4–6 garlic cloves, chopped

a handful of fresh flat-leaf parsley, chopped

1–2 dried peperoncini, crumbled

Dissolve the sugar in the warm water. Add the yeast and stir. Add 2 tablespoons of olive oil. Leave in a warm place for about 10–15 minutes, until the yeast is activated and frothy.

Sift the flour into a large clean bowl. Add the yeasty water and bring together into a dough. Turn it out on to a lightly floured surface and knead until it's smooth, silky and elastic.

Now massage in the remaining ingredients, a few at a time, until fully incorporated through the dough.

Divide the dough into 4 balls and shape into small round loaves. Brush them with the remaining tablespoon of olive oil, cover and set aside in a warm place to prove for about 2 hours.

Preheat the oven to 200°C (400°F), gas mark 6, and bake the rolls for 30–40 minutes. When they're done, they will sound hollow if you tap them on their bottoms.

Leave to cool on wire racks until you're ready to eat them . . . which will probably not be very long.

PIZZETTE "TRUCCHI" CON 3 CONDIMENTI

Small bite-sized "cheat's" pizzas with 3 toppings

Okay. I admit it. I love these little bites so much that I use a ready-made pizza dough. Yes, I know, I know. But let's be honest here. We've all done it. I just can't wait for all that proving and rising. And sometimes a girl's in a hurry and needs some pizza. So shoot me. You can top the *pizzette* with whatever you like, but here are a few suggestions.

MAKES 16–18

2 x 220g (7¾oz) portions ready-made pizza dough (I like Northern Dough Co.), defrosted if frozen

flour, for dusting

Preheat the oven to 240°C (475°F), gas mark 9.

On a lightly floured surface roll the 2 sets of dough out, one at a time, to about 5mm (¼ inch) thick. Using a 6cm (2½ inch) cutter or template, punch out your little *pizzette*. Place them on a floured baking tray.

Top with your choice of the following 3 toppings: Bianche (tomato-free "white" pizza, see opposite), classic Margherita (see page 202) or Diavola e Acciughe (which literally means "Devil and anchovy", see page 203) if you like it hot.

For the topping

olive oil, to drizzle

250g (9oz) buffalo mozzarella cheese

50g (1¾oz) Parmesan cheese, freshly grated

4 sprigs of fresh rosemary, leaves only, chopped

sea salt and freshly ground black pepper

BIANCHE

Drizzle a little oil over each disc of dough.

Rip up the mozzarella and dot evenly over the *pizzette*. Add the rosemary and the Parmesan. Season with salt and pepper.

Add another drizzle of olive oil and bake in the oven (see opposite) for 10–15 minutes, until golden brown and bubbling.

RECIPES CONTINUE OVER THE PAGE

PIZZETTE "TRUCCHI" CON 3 CONDIMENTI

For the topping

olive oil, to drizzle

400g (14oz) can of good-quality chopped tomatoes

1 teaspoon dried oregano

125g (4½oz) buffalo mozzarella cheese

sea salt and freshly ground black pepper

fresh basil, to garnish

MARGHERITA

Drizzle each disc with some olive oil.

Roughly crush up the chopped tomatoes, either with your hands or by pulsing in a food processor – we want some texture. Add the oregano and season with salt and pepper.

Smear the tomato mixture over the *pizzette*. Tear up the mozzarella and dot over evenly. Add another drizzle of oil and bake in the oven (see page 200) for 10–15 minutes.

Garnish with some fresh basil.

For the topping

olive oil, to drizzle

400g (14oz) can of good-quality chopped tomatoes

1 garlic clove, crushed

a good pinch of crushed dried chilli flakes (more if you like it hot)

125g (4½oz) buffalo mozzarella cheese

16–18 anchovies, drained

16–18 pitted black olives, halved (optional)

½ teaspoon dried oregano

sea salt and freshly ground black pepper

DIAVOLA E ACCIUGHE

Drizzle a little olive oil over each disc.

Roughly crush up the chopped tomatoes, either with your hands or by pulsing in a food processor – we want some texture. Add the garlic, chilli flakes and salt and pepper.

Smear the tomato mixture over the *pizzette*. Tear up the mozzarella and scatter over evenly. Drape over the anchovies and dot with the olives, if using. Scatter over the dried oregano. Drizzle with a little more olive oil and bake in the oven (see page 200) for 10–15 minutes.

FARINATA GENOVESE DI CECI

Genoan chickpea pancake

This savoury, chickpea flour pancake is a Genoan speciality, and a perfect drinking snack – crispy on the outside, soft and yielding within. The recipe here is adapted from Marcella Hazan's, which appears in *Marcella Cucina*. (After all, when we're writing about Italian food in English, we all owe a debt to the great Marcella. My husband credits his mum, his Italian landlady and Marcella, via her books, for teaching him to cook.) When I first made this, back in my New York days, I expected the batter to be thicker after its four hours' resting, and slightly freaked out. Do not let this worry you. Marcella, as always, has our backs. It will all work out in the end.

MAKES 12–16 SMALL PIECES

1 teaspoon salt

575ml (1 pint) water

225g (8oz) chickpea (gram) flour

4 tablespoons olive oil

50g (1¾oz) finely sliced onion

1 sprig of fresh rosemary, leaves only

freshly ground black pepper

In a mixing bowl, dissolve the salt in the water. Then sift in the chickpea flour. Add 2 tablespoons of the olive oil and bring the mixture together thoroughly with a fork or a whisk. Leave to stand at room temperature for at least 4 hours.

While the batter is maturing, soak the onions in cold water. Every hour or so, change the water, squeezing out the onions with your hand to remove all their milky sap. After the fourth change, transfer the onions to a little bowl and dress them with 1 tablespoon of the olive oil.

Preheat the oven to 180°C (350°F), gas mark 4.

Add the rosemary leaves to the batter, and stir thoroughly.

You will need a 28 x 18cm (11 x 7 inch) baking tin that's about 5cm (2 inches) deep. Grease the tin with the remaining olive oil, then pour the batter into the tin. Scatter the onions evenly over the top, then bake for 40–50 minutes, or until its edges have turned brown and crisp.

Remove the farinata from its tin, cut it into square diamond-shaped pieces and sprinkle with black pepper.

DOLCI

CROSTATA DI FICHI CON TIMO, FORMAGGIO DI CAPRA E MIELE

Fig tart with thyme, goats' cheese and honey

I have always found it very wise to keep some ready-rolled puff pastry in the fridge or freezer at all times. It allows me to whip up a quick dessert like this at a moment's notice . . .

SERVES 6–8

1 sheet of ready-bought puff pastry, square or round

1 egg, beaten

300g (10½oz) fresh figs, halved or quartered

75g (2¾oz) soft goats' cheese

4 sprigs of fresh thyme, leaves only

1–2 tablespoons olive oil

2 tablespoons caster sugar

a pinch of sea salt

Preheat the oven to 220°C (425°F), gas mark 7.

Lay the puff pastry on a baking tray lined with nonstick baking paper. Then, using a sharp knife, make a cut – not all the way through – down and across each side of the oblong of pastry (or around the round one) about 2cm (¾ inch) in from the edges. This will give the pie a nice crusty raised rim. Brush the pastry with beaten egg.

Place the figs over the pastry, distributing them evenly within the knife cuts. Now dot with the goats' cheese. Scatter with the thyme leaves and drizzle with the olive oil. Sprinkle 1 tablespoon of the sugar over the top, and season with a good pinch of sea salt.

Pop the tart into the oven for about 20 minutes, or until it's golden brown and puffy on the outside, with the figs collapsing slightly and the cheese deliciously melt-y.

Sprinkle with the remaining sugar and serve while it's still hot.

SGROPPINO

Lemon sorbet served with vodka and Prosecco

Sgroppino can be either a drink or a dessert – a simple but delicious beginning or end to a meal, just sharp lemon sorbet and a shot or two of vodka, topped up with some Prosecco. If pressed for time, you can buy a good-quality sorbet; if not, here is my very simple recipe. It makes a lot but it is delicious . . .

MAKES 1 LITRE (1¾ PINTS) OF LEMON SORBET

500g (1lb 2oz) caster sugar

500ml (18fl oz) water

500ml (18fl oz) lemon juice

1 tablespoon lemon zest

To make the sgroppino

1–2 scoops lemon sorbet (see above)

25ml (1fl oz) vodka

Prosecco, to top up

Place the sugar in a large saucepan and add the water. Heat over a low to medium heat until the sugar has completely dissolved. Remove from the heat and leave to cool. Once it's cool, add the lemon juice and the lemon zest and stir.

Churn in an ice-cream maker as per the manufacturer's instructions.

When ready to make the *sgroppino*, place a scoop or two of the sorbet in a dish. Add a shot of vodka, then pour over some Prosecco.

AFFOGATO

Vanilla ice cream with espresso coffee

Could there be a simpler, more grown-up dessert than this? It's as stylish and oh, as Italian as a perfect piece of vintage Gucci. And, thanks to the freshly brewed espresso, it's so hot right now.

SERVES 4

For the vanilla ice cream
285ml (9½fl oz) milk

1 vanilla pod, split, seeds scraped out

4 egg yolks

100g (3½oz) caster sugar

285ml (9½fl oz) double cream

To make the affogato
4–8 scoops of best-quality vanilla ice cream (see above)

4 small cups of espresso coffee

Place the milk in a large saucepan. Add the vanilla pod and seeds. Bring the milk up to the boil but DO NOT let it boil. Remove from the heat and leave to cool completely.

In a large bowl, beat together the egg yolks with the sugar until pale and creamy.

Strain the infused milk through a fine sieve, discarding the vanilla pod.

Add the milk mixture to the egg yolks and stir. Pour the mixture back into the pan and heat very gently. DO NOT boil. Stir until it thickens and coats your spoon. Remove from the heat. Leave to cool.

When it's cold, stir in the double cream. Pour into your ice-cream maker and churn as per the instructions.

Serve the ice cream in the prettiest dishes you have. Have the espresso alongside, or pour the hot coffee over the cold ice cream. Experience deep joy.

TIP: To ring the changes, you could make a cardamom ice cream instead of vanilla. It is utterly delicious, that whiff of coffee and spice whisking one on an olfactory magic carpet to the souks of the Levant. Just replace the vanilla pod with 15 lightly crushed cardamom seeds and make the ice cream exactly as above.

CANTUCCI E VIN SANTO

Almond biscuits with vin santo

Ah . . . *cantucci* – crisp, delicate and studded with almonds. I really think they are the quintessential Italian biscuit. And they make the perfect accompaniment to a cold glass of sweet *vin santo* or "holy wine". Traditionally these wines are from Tuscany and are sweet, nutty and caramelly. Like liquid sunshine . . .

MAKES 25–30

450g (1lb) plain flour

1 teaspoon baking powder

170g (6oz) butter, softened

340g (12oz) caster sugar

3 eggs, plus 1 extra yolk

a good grating of nutmeg (optional)

¼ teaspoon vanilla extract (optional)

225g (8oz) whole unblanched almonds

vin santo, to serve

Preheat the oven to 200°C (400°F), gas mark 6.

Sift together the flour and baking powder and set aside. Cream together the butter and sugar, then add the eggs and egg yolk and beat them in. Add the nutmeg and vanilla, if using, followed by the flour, in thirds, and stir into a batter. Then add the almonds and stir until the batter is smooth and the almonds are incorporated.

Refrigerate for 10 minutes to make the dough easier to handle. Line a baking tray with nonstick baking paper, then shape or pipe on the biscuit mixture as though you're shaping baguettes – you should have 2–3 of them.

Bake the logs of dough in the oven for about 15–20 minutes, until golden and just cooked through. Remove them from the oven, leave to cool slightly, so you can handle them, then cut diagonally into 1cm (½ inch) thick biscuit slices. They will be fragile. Don't worry. Return the biscuits to the oven and bake until golden, about 8–10 minutes.

Cool on a wire rack.

Serve the *cantucci* with as many glasses of *vin santo* as you please . . .

CAFFE CORRETTO

Literally, this means "corrected coffee" – that is, coffee with a drop of the hard stuff. Something to set one up for the day. Or night.

MAKES 1

30ml (1fl oz) grappa

1 small cup of good espresso

Serve the liquor in a small glass alongside the coffee. Add to the coffee at your pleasure. *Salute!*

If you must, you can always replace the grappa with sambuca.

GLOSSARY OF UK & US TERMS

UK	US	UK	US
aubergine	eggplant	grill, to grill	broiler, to broil
baking paper	parchment paper	icing sugar	confectioners' sugar
borlotti beans	cranberry beans	kitchen paper	paper towel
biscuit	cookie	lemon rind	lemon zest
broad beans	fava beans	minced	ground
butter beans	lima beans	passata	tomato puree or sauce
caster sugar	superfine sugar	plain flour	all-purpose flour
celeriac	celery root	prawn	large shrimp
chestnut mushrooms	cremini mushrooms	red or yellow pepper	bell pepper
chickpea flour	gram flour or besan	rocket	arugula
chickpeas	garbanzo beans	single cream	light or pouring cream
chicory	Belgian endive	spring onions	scallions, green onions
clingfilm	plastic wrap	stock	broth
cornflour	cornstarch	sultanas	golden raisins
double cream	heavy cream	sweet peppers	bell peppers
fast-action dried yeast	active dry yeast	tin (roasting, baking)	pan
frying pan	skillet	tomato purée	tomato paste
greaseproof paper	wax paper	vanilla pod	vanilla bean
griddle pan	grill pan	wire rack	cooling rack

BIBLIOGRAPHY

Talia Baiocchi and Leslie Pariseau, *Spritz* (Ten Speed Press, 2016)

Leigh and Nargess Banks, *The Life Negroni* (Spinach Publishing, 2015)

Richard Burr, *BIY: Bake It Yourself* (Quadrille, 2015)

Giancarlo and Katie Caldesi, *Venice: Recipes Lost and Found* (Hardie Grant, 2014)

Elizabeth David, *Italian Food* (MacDonald, 1954, revised 1987)

Emiko Davies, *Florentine* (Hardie Grant, 2016)

Melissa Hamilton and Christopher Hirsheimer, *Canal House Cooks Every Day* (Andrews McMeel, 2012)

Marcella Hazan, *The Classic Italian Cookbook* (Macmillan, 1973, revised 1980)

Marcella Hazan, *Marcella Cucina* (Macmillan, 1997)

Marisa Huff, *Aperitivo: The Cocktail Culture Of Italy* (Rizzoli, 2016)

Pino Luongo, *A Tuscan In The Kitchen* (Clarkson Potter, 1988)

Kay Plunkett-Hogge and John Vincent, *Leon: Family & Friends* (Conran Octopus, 2012)

Gary Regan, *The Negroni: Drinking La Dolce Vita* (Ten Speed Press, 2015)

Rachel Roddy, *Five Quarters: Recipes And Notes from A Kitchen In Rome* (Saltyard Books, 2015)

Delia Smith, *Delia's Summer Collection* (BBC Books, 1993)

Stanley Tucci and Felicity Blunt, with Kay Plunkett-Hogge, *The Tucci Table* (Orion, 2015)

INDEX

ACKNOWLEDGEMENTS

My gosh – another one with the Octopi! You all make birthing a book seem so effortless, and I am ever grateful for all your hard work. Alison Starling, the queen of publishers; Alex Stetter, as thorough an editrix as you could ever hope for; Juliette Norsworthy, director of art, keeper of everything on the straight and narrow; Abi Read, whose illustrations delight always; Naomi Edmondson, designer of dreams; Allison Gonsalves, production guru; Denise Bates, who brooks no nonsense; Kevin Hawkins, sales genius; Caroline Brown, Ellen Bashford, Matt Grindon, Saskia Sidey and Siobhan McDermott, PR freaks – I adore you.

Thank you thank you and thank you again to Tamin Jones and Stephanie Howard for your incredible work on the photographs and for bringing your eating boots to every day of the shoot.

To Fred, Maya, Wilcox, Hepburn, my family – I couldn't do it without you.

And of course, the deepest thanks to all who helped along the way – James Ramsden and Fergus Henderson for competing Negroni variations; Massimo Usai and Susanna Mattana, and the team at Isola del Sole; Musa Özgül, Jeremy Lee and the Hart Brothers at Quo Vadis; Giancarlo and Katie Caldesi; Rebecca Mascarenhas and the staff of Bibo; Jarrett Wrisley and Paolo Vitaletti at Appia (Bangkok); Giuseppi and Pamela Turi at Enoteca Turi; Stanley Tucci and Felicity Blunt; Pepe Mallardo from Guiliano's Deli; Rachel Roddy; Richard Burr; Signor e Signora Ballastrazzi from Massaria Il Frantoio in Ostuni; Gerry's Wine & Spirits, Soho, and John Vincent at Leon.

Grazie mille!

An Hachette UK Company
www.hachette.co.uk

First published in Great Britain
in 2017 by Mitchell Beazley,
a division of Octopus Publishing Group Ltd
Carmelite House, 50 Victoria Embankment
London EC4Y 0DZ
www.octopusbooks.co.uk

Text Copyright © Kay Plunkett-Hogge 2017

Design, illustrations & photography © Octopus Publishing Group Ltd 2017

Distributed in the US by
Hachette Book Group
1290 Avenue of the Americas
4th and 5th Floors
New York, NY 10104

Distributed in Canada by
Canadian Manda Group
664 Annette St.
Toronto, Ontario, Canada M6S 2C8

ISBN 978 1 78472 310 1

A CIP catalogue record for this book is available from the British Library.

Printed and bound in China

10 9 8 7 6 5 4 3 2 1

Publisher: Alison Starling
Senior Editor: Alex Stetter
Art Director: Juliette Norsworthy
Designer: Naomi Edmondson
Photography: Tamin Jones
Illustrations: Abigail Read
Senior Production Controller: Allison Gonsalves